How to Work in Denmark

Tips on finding a job, succeeding at work,
and understanding your Danish boss

Kay Xander Mellish

Forlag: BoD – Books on Demand, Hellerup, Danmark
Tryk: BoD – Books on Demand, Norderstedt, Tyskland

ISBN: 9788743048688

Contents

Introduction: The good news about working in Denmark

If you're feeling underpaid, under-challenged, or stressed out in your current employment market, there are a lot of good reasons to work in Denmark.

Working hours are reasonable, giving you plenty of time with your family if you have one and more time for hobbies and friends if you don't.

Denmark's high-tech, high-end industries offer plenty of quality projects, plus the resources and equipment to get them done right.

Salaries are good, too, although a large chunk of your income will go to taxes and housing costs, particularly in Aarhus and Copenhagen.

The famous Danish social welfare state will provide for your basic medical care as soon as you arrive. Once you spend some time in the country, you'll also be eligible for free further-education courses or even a master's degree.

A good place to raise a family

If you have children, you'll find the primary school system to be high-quality and low-pressure, with an emphasis on emotional intelligence and the practical use of knowledge.

Should you be considering starting a family, you and your partner will be offered up to a year of paid time off, split between you, to spend time with your new baby.

Once that year is over, you'll be able to choose from a variety of subsidized, low-cost daycare options. Good daycare means that a large percentage of Danish women work outside the home and are able to advance in their careers.

It's also a requirement that all salaried employees be given at least five full weeks of vacation per year, in addition to the numerous Danish public holidays clustered around Christmas and in the spring.

Who wouldn't want to work in Denmark?

Difficult weather, difficult friendships

Still, Denmark sometimes has trouble attracting internationals, for a number of reasons.

The weather is reliably awful: in some years, the gray, rainy spring continues right through summer. If you haven't experienced wearing a Puffa jacket and gloves in June where you live, you'll probably get that chance in Denmark.

From October through March, the Danish nights are dark and long. Without an absorbing hobby or a good circle of friends, internationals can feel isolated and alone.

And making friends can be hard. Danes treasure the life-long friendships they made back in their school days but aren't always good at reaching out to newcomers and building new relationships.

A hungry tax system

Denmark's hungry tax system is also a turn-off for some internationals. For the most part, you'll pay into it for years without being able to draw much out of it.

On my website, "How to Live in Denmark," I frequently get questions from internationals impressed by Danish salary levels and wondering how much they will be able to save and take home after a couple of years in Denmark.

The answer is usually not much.

The top income tax rate is near 50% for the highest earners – and around 30% for the lowest. (In Denmark, everybody pays income tax, even the unemployed.) There's also a 25% sales tax imposed on most items you'll purchase, including food.

While your visits to the doctor are free, the medicine your doctor prescribes is usually not. Dental care for adults is only partially covered and tends to be quite expensive; sometimes the bills can be more painful than the treatment.

Transport is expensive too. A monthly train or bus pass can be a substantial item in your budget, depending on how far you travel. Cars and motorcycles are taxed at 85% of their purchase price – 150% for luxury models – and fuel is heavily taxed as well.

The social welfare state that makes Denmark a pleasant place to live is expensive, and as a resident of Denmark, you will be helping to pay for it.

The headache of changing immigration rules

Denmark is constantly changing the rules and regulations for newcomers to Denmark, changes that affect non-EU and non-EEA immigrants in particular.

That means immigrants from the USA, Australia, China, India, Africa, and Latin America get caught up in ever-changing requirements for language-learning, test-taking, and length-of-stay requirements before permanent residence is granted.

The ugly truth is that highly-educated internationals are hostages to an ongoing battle about immigration to Denmark, much of which focuses on less-educated newcomers and their paths toward becoming an active part of Danish society. International agreements make it impossible to demand more of one group without demanding more of the other.

People who come here to work find the system exasperating: they never seem to know from one month to the next what the requirements for remaining in Denmark will be. Even marrying a Dane won't guarantee you the right to stay in Denmark these days.

What the companies say

Businesses hate these constant changes too, since the last thing they want is to train a talented employee and then have to worry about their residence permit expiring because they failed to comply with some new rule.

And make no mistake – Denmark dearly needs foreign workers.

It needs highly-educated IT specialists and engineers for its technical and pharmaceutical industries: Danish universities simply don't produce enough graduates to meet the demand.

It needs healthcare workers to deal with an aging population where the elderly are cared for by the welfare system, not their families.

It needs hospitality workers to staff the tourist trade. (In particular, Denmark is very popular with Chinese tourists, who grew up with the stories of Hans Christian Andersen.)

And it needs agricultural workers to help slaughter the thousands of pigs that supply the world with Danish bacon and pick the exquisitely flavorful strawberries, cherries, and apples that grow during Denmark's short harvest season.

The bottom line is, as a foreign worker, you are a critical part of the Danish economy. Denmark would have a hard time functioning without you. Welcome.

Part 1: Getting the job

Why job titles aren't that important in Denmark

When I make presentations to groups of internationals who have come to work in Denmark, I generally ask for just a few simple items – a screen, a remote control for the projector, and a glass of water.

On a recent gig, I was provided with everything except the water. Since I had met several of the company's Danish employees when I arrived – handshakes with Mette, Søren, and Nikolaj – I asked one of them to kindly get me a glass of water. I asked Nikolaj.

Nikolaj smiled, walked off, and brought me back a glass of water.

It was only after the presentation was finished and I was at home making connections on LinkedIn that I found out that Nikolaj was Senior Vice President for Europe, with more than 650 people working under him and a salary that must have been in the three million-kroner-a-year zone.

But Nikolaj had never mentioned his title to me, because that's just not done in Denmark.

Passion for equality

One of the most important words in the Danish language is *ligestilling* – equality. The belief that all (Danish) people are basically equal permeates every relationship and every interaction.

(It's one of the reasons customer service tends to be so poor in Denmark – there's no tradition of anyone serving anyone else.)

You could dig deep into Danish history to find the reason for this passion for equality, which probably has something to do with the need for farmers and fishermen to co-operate in order to make it through the dark Scandinavian winters.

Fancy job titles do not fit that passion for equality. They suggest that you think you're better than someone else. Which you might actually be if you've worked your way to the top of your field, but that admission is slightly embarrassing.

Janteloven ("Jante law"), the informal but ubiquitous Danish social code, forbids the display of any kind of status.

No titles on office doors

If you do have an impressive job title, it's considered bad taste to show it off.

For example, office doors in Denmark often have just the name of the person inside, not their title. When you introduce yourself, whether to one person or an audience of 500, you give just your name, preferably your first name. (Like Nikolaj did.)

And it's considered laughable to strut about in a way that shows everyone you're the boss.

In fact, when you enter a room full of Danish businesspeople, it is almost impossible to tell who the boss is. Everyone's dressed the same, everyone acts pretty much the same, and nobody shows any particular deference to the boss.

This can be a problem when you're a job hunter or salesperson and have to figure out who in the room has the power to make a decision.

Just the first name

To Danes, titles are pompous. Even surgeons and professors

use their first names in a spoken context or casual written communication.

But the lack of titles can be confusing to foreigners who do business with Danes. Many people, particularly those from hierarchical cultures, want to deal with a Dane of a similar status as their own.

When Danes at the top of the educational or corporate ladder sign an email with just their first names – as is considered good, equal manners in Denmark – people from hierarchical societies often assume they're talking to a secretary or an intern.

Danes and the competitive world

For a Dane, titles are a bit like putting on a costume at a party. Titles seem artificial and make them feel slightly uncomfortable. When people from other cultures proudly reel off their elaborate titles (the Germans are specialists at this), the Danes find it tiresome and pretentious.

The truth is, Danes don't always understand how competitive the world outside Denmark can be.

In the USA, India, and China, the competition to get into the "best" schools is brutal and begins in childhood. A "good" primary school may be necessary in order to access a "good" secondary school, which can set you up for a "good" university.

If you outperform everyone else at all three, you might get a chance at a "good" job at a "good" company and then work your way up to a fancy title.

That fancy title means your hard work has paid off. It means you've won.

Having grown up in a welfare state with an extensive safety net, it can be hard for Danes to comprehend how important it is to "win" and how far and fast you can fall if you don't.

Creating a network is more important than showing off

In Denmark, it's much less common to obsess about the "top" primary schools or "top" secondary schools. There are only a few universities, each of which is "top" in its own field.

Throughout the Danish educational system, the focus is on group work, not individual excellence. Successful students focus on building the network they'll need to get good student jobs and internships in their fields – not antagonizing people by showing they're the smartest ones around.

(Danes who have the "smartest one around" type of personality often end up leaving Denmark; I know of several who now run successful businesses in the US.)

Chat about teams, projects, customers, and goals

Anyway, Danes doing business in Denmark don't start a conversation with a potential new contact by asking about titles. They chat about teams, projects, customers, goals, and maybe past companies they've worked for. If a title is mentioned at all, it's mentioned at the end of the conversation.

To be fair, the flat management structure at Danish companies means someone's title doesn't always reflect how much power they have or their ability to hire or sign on the dotted line.

Or whether or not they'll be asked to fetch a visiting American a glass of water.

Fine-tuning your approach to the Danish job market

The Danish workplace has a flat structure, which means you're unlikely to find a position in which a boss tells you to do something, and you do it, and then the boss tells you to do something else, and you do that.

In Denmark, a boss is more of a coach or team leader-type figure. He or she gets power not from a position or a title but by being able to rally the people on a team to do good work.

Danish companies are looking for people who can take the initiative and solve problems without being told what to do every step of the way.

And because Denmark is a small country without a vast reserve of labor, you will need to be flexible on the job, ready to take on challenges that might not be exactly what you were hired for.

"They can't think for themselves"

When Danish employers talk about foreign workers behind their backs, they often whisper, "They can't think for themselves."

This isn't true, of course, but if your home country's work culture involves a hands-on boss who directs your every move, you might need to fine-tune your approach to the Danish job market.

If you want a job in Denmark, you need to show that you understand a company's needs and that you can come up with some fresh ideas to help them address those needs.

You have to turn up with a lot of ideas and enthusiasm, and act as if you're not just looking for a job, but a professional challenge.

How do I get from my home country to Denmark?

Many Danish companies advertise their top job openings online and in English. You can apply directly from wherever you live. Headhunters and recruiters in your home country might also have branches in Denmark; get in touch and see if they can help.

It's not necessary to speak Danish in your initial approach to the Danish job market, although it will be helpful if you actually find yourself moving to Denmark.

Some entry-level serving jobs in bars and restaurants are also okay with hiring people who do not speak Danish, and so are trendy shops that cater to a younger target group.

Nordic and EU citizens

Your next hurdle, however, will be the work permit process, which depends on your citizenship.

Citizens of the Nordic countries – Norway, Sweden, Finland, and Iceland – can live and work in Denmark at any time and with very little fuss. (They don't even need a passport to enter the country.)

Citizens of the European Union, meanwhile, can simply show up in Denmark and begin working, although they will need to go through the formality of applying for a residence permit after three months. EU citizens can also live in Denmark for up to six months while looking for a job.

The non-Nordic, non-EU applicant

The tricky part comes if you are neither a Nordic citizen

nor an EU citizen. You will need a permit to work in Denmark, which isn't always easy to achieve. In most cases, a company will need to sponsor you.

These sponsorships are a little bit easier if what you do for a living is on the "positive list," which is a list of professions experiencing a shortage of workers in Denmark. The positive list is updated every six months – do a search for "positive list Denmark" to find the latest version.

In addition, researcher jobs and high-paying jobs are currently "fast-tracked" in the Danish worker visa program, which is designed to help Denmark bring in top people from around the world.

Otherwise, you will be at the mercy of Denmark's SIRI immigration agency, which will put you and your potential employer through a more or less arduous process to get you the approvals you need.

Bigger Danish companies tend to have more HR people accustomed to dealing with the work permit system and often have a dedicated contact person at SIRI, which oils the wheels of the approval process.

Getting your first approval, with the weight of an eager company behind you, is often easier than getting subsequent approvals if you decide to stay in Denmark.

How do you know which companies to apply to?

Your first stop to learn about any field in Denmark is the union for that field. (You can read more about unions in the chapter *Is joining a union worth it?*)

Do an online search and find out which union in Denmark takes care of your particular field. The Danish word for union is *fagforening*, which is different from an *A-kasse*, although they are often run by the same group of people. (Unless you're already in Denmark as a student, you don't need an *A-kasse* until you have a Danish job.)

If you need to transfer professional qualifications from your home country, the union can tell you how to do it.

Reading the Danish trade press

Your second stop is the trade press about your field. For example, in the IT field, it's ComputerWorld.dk; for engineers, it's ING.dk; for the life science industry, Medwatch.com; if you're in advertising, check out Bureaubiz.dk.

A lot of this press is in Danish, but Google Translate will help. See which companies are in your field, who's doing well and who is firing people. Don't forget start-ups, which are often quite open to hiring newcomers. Find out if there are certain skills in your field that Danish companies need, and then focus on these skills as you market yourself.

Think about past projects you've done that demonstrate your most valuable skills. Danes are always more impressed by projects and results than they are by degrees and certificates.

Show off your expertise on social media

Follow the trade press and the companies you're targeting on social media, in particular LinkedIn and Facebook. When there's a story that addresses a topic you know something about, post an intelligent, information-rich comment using your real name.

This will get your name in front of the people in your industry who might be interested in hiring someone like you. Do this on a regular basis so you start to build momentum.

Commenting in English is fine, even if the original post is in Danish – but it should be very good English.

When I write in Danish, I always cut and paste the text into a Microsoft Word document to check for major spelling and grammatical errors; you can try the same technique for English. The free plug-in Grammarly can help as well.

Personalize your connection request

If someone responds to your comment, thank them and add additional information if you can, and then send them a connection request on LinkedIn – personalized to say how you know their name and what value you can offer them if they connect with you.

Never send the standardized connection request. I get dozens of these every day, some of them from people in faraway countries who have no clear reason to connect with me, and I just delete them.

The goal is to build a network

The goal is to build a network and build yourself as a brand name in your industry. Denmark needs people with your expertise – now you just have to show people what you can offer. And you can start doing this before you even arrive in Denmark.

Putting together your Danish CV

I've applied for jobs in Denmark and been hired. I've also been the person doing the hiring and sorting through applications.

Here's the truth: it's really no fun on either side. On the applicant side, you can feel like a beggar, desperate for someone to recognize and reward your talent. It wears on your confidence, particularly in a long hiring process, which is common in Denmark even for Danes.

On the hiring side, you're facing a huge stack of applications, mostly from people who know nothing about the company, nothing about the job, and are sending you a standardized letter or CV that doesn't reveal anything about why they're a good fit.

For example, when I was hiring for a copyediting position at a financial company in Copenhagen, I got a letter in flawless English from a woman who was a display artist at IKEA. She put together the sofas and pillows to give the imitation living rooms a chic and homey atmosphere. It's noble work, but it had absolutely nothing to do with the job we had advertised, and she'd given no indication of how her skills would transfer.

Highlight the projects you've worked on

So, that application got trashed, and so will yours if you don't take the time to explain why you're the right person to work at this particular company in that particular job. It's not really the employer's role to look through your CV (or resumé, as North Americans say) and imagine how you might fit with the position on offer. It's your role to show why you're right for the position and how you can start adding value right away.

That's why I recommend having a Danish CV that highlights the projects you've worked on and how your contributions to those projects relate to the job you want.

For example, an acquaintance of mine who was applying for an administrative job had a degree in Elizabethan literature, but she'd also spent several years as a volunteer event planner at her son's school.

Even though it was unpaid, the second role had more relevance to the job she wanted since it involved scheduling, budgets, dealing with suppliers, and juggling a wide variety of stakeholders and egos. I encouraged her to go into detail about this organizational experience on her CV.

A bitter pill to swallow

Unless you are a senior hire with a complex career, your Danish CV shouldn't be more than one or two pages – and the most exciting information should be on the first page, where an overwhelmed hiring manager can easily find it. Personally, I rarely read past the first page, particularly when office-job applicants used the later pages to go into detail about restaurant and babysitting jobs they held decades ago.

Keeping things short means you have to decide which aspects of your experience to emphasize. It can be a bitter pill to swallow that the things you are most proud of may not be things Danish employers care about.

Titles and grades and exam results (unless they're required for the job, as they are for accountants, architects, and engineers) aren't a golden ticket to employment in

Denmark, even if you've attended an excellent school.

That's why it's so important to explain exactly what you *did* at each of your jobs and how you can do that and more for a new employer. Most Danish employers are looking for someone who is plug-and-play – someone who can do the job on their first day at work and be a good social fit on the team.

Highlight your openness to Danish culture

Social fit is another thing that Danish employers worry about when hiring internationals. As much as they need internationals' skills (particularly in the technical industries) and as much as they want to see themselves as culturally relaxed and open, most Danes grew up in a monoculture where there is a certain Danish way of doing things, and they worry that you may not know what that is.

Make no mistake: if asked to choose between a technically excellent employee who won't fit into the team and a less gifted employee who will, Danish hiring managers will choose the second employee every time. Teamwork and group work are extraordinarily important to Danish society.

If you're not Danish, you don't have to pretend you are, but showing your openness to Danish culture and the Danish way of doing things will be a point in your favor.

For example, indicate how far you've come in your Danish-language classes, or that you're studying Danish online with a program like Duolingo. If you've been living in Denmark for a while and have been involved in sports clubs (such as a running club) or community activities (like a parent board at your child's kindergarten) make sure to add that too.

If you're entirely new to Denmark, read up on it and be ready to talk about why you might want to work in Denmark as opposed to anyplace else on the globe. A little humor here is okay: the Danes know that they have terrible weather, and that you will probably be taking a step down in the sunny-days-per-year department if you come from anyplace but Britain.

Choose a photo that makes you look friendly

A Danish CV generally includes a photo, although one is not required. I've noticed that people from cultures in which work is a serious business tend to choose photos in which they are grim, unsmiling, and wearing their most formal work clothing, a bit like a passport photo.

This is the wrong approach for Denmark. Your Danish CV photo – which can also be your LinkedIn photo – should show you smiling slightly, as if you don't take yourself too seriously, an admired trait in Denmark. You should look as if you'd be a pleasant person to share a coffee break with.

Invest in a good photo. In an era where nearly everyone has a smartphone, there is no excuse for a badly-lit or blurry one, or one in which you are in wedding attire. Hire a pro if you can, or do a quick "modeling session" on a sunny day with a friend as a photographer.

Alternatively, you can choose a photo that shows you on the job – a surveyor on a construction site wearing a hard hat, or a nurse in a hospital setting.

A nickname the Danes can handle

Your name is something to be proud of; it reflects your identity and your culture. There's also a good chance that

Danes won't know how to pronounce it.

A wonderful feature on LinkedIn allows you to make a short recording that demonstrates the correct pronunciation of your name.

Alternatively, consider using your initials, finding a Danish equivalent to your name (*Steffen* from *Stjepan*), or just coming up with a nickname the Danes can handle.

Having something short and pronounceable is particularly useful when calling on the telephone; for example, my advice to a Lithuanian job applicant named *Ovidijus* was that on the telephone, he should be *Ove*. *Ove* has the extra advantage of being an actual Danish name, although an old-fashioned one. Some Chinese speakers coming to Denmark choose a Danish nickname for their time here, much as Westerners choose Chinese names when doing business in China.

You don't have to do this, although it's certainly an attention-getter to see a Danish name like *Mette* or *Magnus* in the middle of a given name and surname that is clearly Asian or African.

At any rate, if you've provided some assistance to the Danes in pronouncing your name, you've removed one small hurdle to your advancement in the Danish job market.

Avoid stupid copyediting mistakes

It goes without saying that your CV should be in flawless English. You want your employer to focus on your excellent skill set, not that you failed to capitalize the name of your university or that you've typed three mysterious commas in a row (,,,). I've seen both of these mistakes, and many, many, more, on the resumés of disappointed job seekers.

Get a pro to check your CV before sending it out. On-line services like Fiverr.com and Upwork.com have plenty of people ready to do this for a relatively small investment.

Your Danish cover letter and LinkedIn profile, plus two magic words

In the era of online applications, face-to-face networking, and LinkedIn profiles, the Danish cover letter is a bit of a lost art.

Probably your future employer will "meet" you via one of these other channels before they ever read the letter that is supposedly introducing you.

But it's still worth writing because it's a chance to set the experience on your CV into the context of the job on offer.

For example, I met a woman who had spent her entire career in network infrastructure industry – and really wanted to try something else. Although her CV showed one network infrastructure job after another, her cover letter was a great place to explain why she was applying for a job in a different industry and how her experience could be useful there.

A good cover letter is particularly useful if you're a new arrival in Denmark, a new graduate, or going for a job that isn't an obvious fit with what you've already done. It's also a good place to explain how your particular education and experience would be a good match for this job.

Keep it short and talk about Denmark

Your letter should be short, direct, and without mistakes in grammar and spelling. A flawless cover letter gives you a chance to show you care about thoroughness and quality, both of which are points of pride in Denmark.

Three short paragraphs should be enough to describe who you are and why you want *this* job with *this* company.

If you're newly arrived in Denmark, you can also use your cover letter to explain why you chose this country over others. Danes love their country and are proud of it; it certainly won't hurt to show that you like it too and are not just an opportunist who will take a job anywhere as long as it offers a fat paycheck. And if you're willing to relocate within Denmark for the job, say so.

The traditional Danish letter style dispenses with tired openers like "Dear Sirs/Madams." Instead, it has a subject line on top, a bit like an email. You can use this to your advantage. A line like **Experienced social media copywriter with proven high conversion rates** is certainly a more eye-catching start to a letter than the old-fashioned "To Whom It May Concern."

Chat with the hiring manager if you can

Let's scroll back for a minute, though. As I said, the cover letter is probably not your first encounter with an employer.

Many Danish job ads contain the phone number of the hiring manager, who is often the exact person you will be working for if you get the job.

This is an opportunity for you to call, introduce yourself, and ask an intelligent question about the job. (Yeah, an intelligent question – nothing that's already in the job description or something you can find out on the company's website.)

Please, please find a quiet room where your future employer can hear what you are saying – I have had people call me from train stations with trains whizzing by or from coffee shops with the latest Beyoncé hit pumping in the background.

Approach the hiring manager along these lines: "*This is (your name here). I understand that you're the hiring manager for the (job name), and I'm interested, but I have a couple of questions. Is now a good time?"*

Assuming the hiring manager is not halfway through her lunch or on her way to a meeting, you can then take five or ten minutes of her time to ask a few questions that are directly relevant to the position, such as the team structure, travel requirements, or management responsibilities.

Please ask about things that relate to the work at hand, not whether you can get off early on Fridays because you play tennis or if it's okay that you already have a vacation planned for the company's busiest season.

If the answers (and the boss) are to your liking, you can reference the conversation in the first paragraph of your cover letter. Just to make sure the contact is fresh in her memory, I recommend sending your application within 24 hours of having spoken to the hiring manager.

Polish your LinkedIn profile like a diamond

Before you write your cover letter and before you approach a hiring manager, you should have your LinkedIn profile in order. When it comes to social media, Danes use Instagram and Facebook for social purposes and are indifferent about Twitter, but they love LinkedIn.

Anyone who is serious about doing business and finding a job in Denmark should polish his or her LinkedIn profile like a diamond.

An excellent business profile photo is a must. Your "headline"– the job title that goes right below your name – should be packed full of the kind of search words recruiters will type in when they're looking for someone like you. The more specific, the better.

I get so mad when I see someone who has just written

"Engineer" in the headline field. No, you're an *Environmental engineer specializing in wastewater purification.*

On the other hand, don't throw a bunch of unrelated job concepts in the headline: *Copywriter/Marketer/SEO Expert/ Videographer/Drone Pilot/Tango Dancer/Cook.*

This makes it look as if you'll do anything for money but aren't particularly strong at any specific skill.

Share details about your previous jobs

When it comes to your previous jobs, don't just list your title and dates of employment. Go into details about the projects you've worked on and the products, materials, and teams you've worked with. Tell a little story about your time on the job and what you learned there. LinkedIn profiles don't have to be a dry collection of bullet points.

LinkedIn even has a great "portfolio" feature that lets you post documentation of the work you've already done. Photos, articles that you've written or have been written about you, videos, short project summaries, charts – anything colorful or visual.

This helps make your work experience come alive and seem more concrete, particularly if most of it consists of work done outside of Denmark.

Short updates help establish your brand

LinkedIn also allows you to post short updates, which you can use to share information about what's going on in your field.

These posts put your name in the news feeds of all the great new industry contacts you'll build up during the first phase of your job search. They keep your name fresh in their minds for when they need to fill a job. If you're a gifted writer, you can even write a longer LinkedIn post about some topic of interest in your business. This helps establish you as a local "expert."

I also recommend video updates – just you speaking directly into your phone about whatever is going on in your field. Videos give you a chance to show off your personality and confirm that your spoken English is clear and understandable, something Danes worry about when they hire from outside Denmark.

Make sure to deliver valuable information to your readers. I frequently see people post scans of their new educational certificates on LinkedIn, or low-resolution photos of the backs of the audience's heads at a presentation they recently delivered.

Don't do this. Your business contacts want to know about new products, new companies, new methods, and new ideas. Asking a question at the end of your post – *What's your best tip for improving conversion rates?* – can produce comments that will bump you up in the algorithm and show your update to more people.

Bottom line: there's a good chance your future employers will find you via your LinkedIn profile. Even if they don't, the hiring manager will probably look at your profile after he or she reviews your CV and cover letter.

Two magic words

When I give presentations to job hunters in Denmark, I tell them there are two words you can add to your cover letter that will guarantee that it will be carefully read.

What are those two words?

The first and last name of someone you know who already works at the company.

Of course, you should only use a current employee's name with his or her permission and ask each time you use it. There's always a chance that your contact and this particular hiring manager are bitter enemies, or that the company is so vast that a recommendation from a scientist won't have much impact on the hiring of an accountant.

But if your contact is working in the same or a similar department, knows the company's culture and priorities, and thinks you're a good fit, the hiring manager will at least take the time to look through your application and see if she agrees.

At the very least, she'll feel she might have to explain to her colleague why she doesn't agree. Denmark is a small job market, so people are careful not to offend their business contacts.

That means your letter and CV will get a little extra attention.

The Danish job interview

I f you've been asked for a job interview at a Danish company, congratulations. Danes don't like to waste time, so they wouldn't be taking time to meet you if they didn't think there was a chance they might hire you.

Job interviewing in Denmark is a difficult balance, because *Janteloven* makes all forms of bragging or self-promotion distasteful to the Danes. You've got to convince the person interviewing you that you're skilled and capable without sounding like a used car salesman.

Think about your successes and failures

I tell potential hires to prepare by reviewing their working history and coming up with three good stories about projects they've worked on – two in which they did well and succeeded, and one that went badly but helped them learn important professional lessons.

By admitting to some mistakes in your work life, you'll give yourself a lot more credibility with Danish companies, who are skeptical of anyone presenting themselves as too perfect.

Danes like to have fun at work and laugh at themselves. If you seem too uptight, they may think you won't be a "good fit" on their otherwise cheerful team.

Come prepared with detailed stories

Your primary preparation for the interview should be thinking through your career and some of the challenges you've faced, particularly the ones that relate to this particular job.

Think in terms of projects and of problem solving. Danish employers want to know how you'll use your independent smarts to tackle challenges, not just wait for a boss to tell you what to do. Details are good, especially if they show your grasp of the nuts and bolts of your industry.

It's also a good idea to re-examine the human qualities listed in the job ad – precision, people skills, or whatever – and arrive at the interview ready to talk about real-life examples that show you possess these qualities.

Lots and lots of handshakes

Danes love punctuality, so do everything you can to be on time for your interview. Danish industrial companies tend to be located on the outskirts of town, and if a bus goes there it often goes once only every half hour, so for heaven's sake plan out your route in advance. Better to be 20 minutes early and kill time in reception than be racing through the door ten minutes late, sweating and swearing.

When you meet the hiring manager, shake his hand and make direct eye contact. Should he introduce you to more people, do the same for each of them – reach out your hand (even if you have to awkwardly reach across a table to do so), say your name clearly, and make eye contact. The Danes see eye contact as a sign of trustworthiness and confidence.

The hiring manager will probably offer some tea or coffee. In bigger companies, this might be delivered to the interview room on a tray, but in smaller companies you may be taken to the group kitchen and told to pour your own hot beverage out of a machine, just like the current employees do.

You can expect some small talk while all this is going on,

so if you're not the naturally chatty type, it can be useful to come pre-equipped with some comments about the weather, the difference between Danish weather and your home country's weather, or similar non-controversial topics.

Once you sit down, your Danish job interviewer may try to warm up the conversation with a few questions about your family or personal life, mostly to get a sense of you as an individual and gauge how committed you are to staying in Denmark. Stick to brief generalities here; there's no need to disclose any information that is too personal.

In particular, women don't need to answer questions about when or whether they plan to have children; this question is illegal. "I'm loving my freedom right now," or "For the moment, I'm just focused on my career," are classic ways to swerve around it.

Avoid a beggar's mentality

Then comes the main part of the interview, where you will be asked about how your qualifications match the job. While you shouldn't be arrogant, you shouldn't have a beggar's mentality, either. These people are taking time out of their busy day because they can't run their business without someone like you.

Approach the interview like a business deal: do both parties have something to offer each other? One researcher found that foreign applicants were often rejected for a job because they seemed too submissive in the interview process; the Danish hiring manager didn't think they'd be able to stand up for themselves in the Danish work environment, which requires initiative and independent thinking.

Personality test and police documents

The company may also ask you to bring a copy of your *straffeattest*, which is a document you can get from the Danish police showing that you have never been convicted of a crime in Denmark. This is particularly likely if the job will involve dealing with money, confidential information, or children.

Don't take this request personally; every candidate for the job will have to do this, including Danes. You can order your *straffeattest* online from the citizen service borger.dk.

In addition, the Danish employer may ask you to take an online personality test. These popular tests can be your friend because they're designed to highlight personal characteristics that are important on the job.

In other words, they counteract the tendency for the hiring manager to just pick somebody she went to school with in Denmark and urge her to look seriously at you, a new arrival who may be more qualified.

Sometimes the test results will be part of the interview. You and the interviewer may discuss how well your personality matches the job. For example: "I see that you're a quiet, introverted personality. Do you think you'll enjoy the sales aspects of this position?"

What should you wear to the interview?

Foreigners looking for jobs in Denmark tend to be overly formal in both dress and manner, which feeds into the Danish prejudice that non-Danish workers are stiff and robot-like.

Before the interview, look at the company's website and see what the people pictured are wearing, and then come dressed like that.

Should you follow up after the interview?

There's a lot of disagreement about the extent to which you should follow up after a job interview.

Personally, I think a brief email the next day is a nice touch. Saying *tak for sidst* ("Thanks for our most recent meeting") and adding a couple short bullet points about why you are right for the job is a way of showing a sincere interest. This is also a good time to supply any additional information the interviewer asked for during your meeting.

Then – leave it alone. If they're interested, you will hear from them within a couple of weeks, certainly less than a month. And if they do get in touch, you may just be at the beginning of a long hiring process that could include more interviews, more tests, and weird inexplicable delays.

This is standard practice. The hiring process when I joined Danske Bank took more than three months, which I later learned was because HR thought I was a poor fit for the job, despite the hiring manager's insistence. The hiring manager won, and I enjoyed working at Danske Bank for many years.

You got the job!

If you do get a job offer in Denmark, congratulations!

Start-ups will probably want you to begin work immediately; larger companies may give you a few weeks or even a couple of months to prepare to get settled and ready, or to go through the work permit process if required.

Your company will give you a contract to sign. Keep in mind that if you're a member of a union, you can have the union's legal team review the contract to make sure it's fair to you.

Your employer won't be surprised or offended by this – it's standard practice – and it's a particularly good idea if you're handed a contract that's all in Danish.

Remember that if something goes wrong on the job, it's your union that will have your back. The Danish government doesn't get involved in workplace disputes.

Is joining a union worth it? (And what's the difference between a union and an *A-kasse?*)

When you first arrive in Denmark to work or look for work, the last thing you need is another monthly expense. So many foreigners "save money" by not joining a union.

I was one of them. To be honest, joining a union never even occurred to me.

In the US, unions are either for manual workers – steelworkers, electricians, hotel housekeeping – or for civil servants, like teachers and cops. Knowledge workers and creative types are almost never unionized.

But that's not true in Denmark, where engineers, doctors, lawyers, bankers, managers, and writers regularly join unions.

Unions can be even more important for foreign employees than they are for Danes.

Access to people who know how things work

First of all, when you join a union, you get access to their specialists. These people speak Danish, they know the Danish salary levels, and they know the Danish social welfare system.

So when you receive a contract from a Danish company, your union can go through the contract and make sure that you're getting a fair deal when it comes to salary and benefits. They can look at vacation time, parental leave benefits, arrangements for your spouse, and other aspects of the contract to see if there are any red flags that you can negotiate away before you sign.

Danish employers expect this. They won't be annoyed if you ask for a day or two to review the contract with your union. The person hiring you probably did this herself before she took her job. It's completely normal.

When it all goes wrong on the job

Secondly, if things don't go as expected on the job, the union can be your backup. When you have a dispute with your employer, you can feel pretty vulnerable as a foreigner – especially if your residence permit depends on your job.

Your union can get involved and can tell you what your rights are. Sometimes they'll even meet with you and your employer to get things sorted out.

And if you lose your job, which happens regularly to both Danes and foreigners, then you really need a union.

The famous "flexicurity" system in Denmark means it's relatively easy to let go of people, particularly if they've worked at a company for less than a year. You can be laid off (or, as the Danes insist on saying, "fired") without having done anything wrong. Maybe the company is changing strategy or simply having a bad year. And off you go.

What happens when you get fired

When you're let go in Denmark – which has happened to me more than once – they call you into a conference room that generally only contains two people: one who tells you that you no longer have a job, plus one to serve as a witness.

And the first question they'll ask you is, "Are you a member of a union?" If you're a union member, you'll have the right to have a fourth person in the room, a union representative who is on your side. That person can make sure you get the best possible departure package.

I was not a member of a union the first time I got laid off, which was why I basically got whatever the company was legally required to give me but nothing more.

On a subsequent layoff, I was indeed a member and was able to call on the union's legal team to decide if it was worth filing a lawsuit against my former employer. (It wasn't.)

Which union should you join?

You'll need to do a little research to find out which union suits you best. Some unions represent specific fields: *IDA* represents engineers, *Pharmadanmark* represents life science people, *Finansforbundet* is for people who work for banks or in the finance industry, and *Lederne* is for managers in any industry.

The good thing about this type of union is that they know your industry well and have a good overview of job prospects and new companies within the sector.

Industry-specific unions also hold networking events where you can meet other people in your field, including people who work at companies that might be future employers. This is why it can sometimes be worth joining these unions even before you get to Denmark, or getting in contact as soon as you arrive.

Unions can help make sure you get paid

There are also unions that cover several fields, the "super unions" like *3F*, *Dansk Metal*, and *HK*.

They can't offer much industry information, so I only recommend joining these if you work at a company that has a specific contract with them. For example, you might be doing student work as a restaurant server or hotel cleaner at a place that has a deal with, for example, 3F.

Because there is no legal minimum wage in Denmark, the *de facto* minimum wage is whatever these unions negotiate with the employer group. So, if your workplace has a deal with 3F, you get the wage agreed on with 3F.

Your union will also help out if you get hurt on the job or if the employer decides not to pay you for some reason – something that happens regularly to vulnerable newcomers, if the Facebook and Reddit groups catering to internationals in Denmark can be believed.

If you've got no union, you've got no backup. The Danish police don't get involved with employee/employer disputes.

Check online ratings of discount unions

The big "super-unions" have been losing members over the past decade or so. Some people feel the monthly membership fees for these unions are too high; others don't like the way the super-unions always seem to line up behind the same Danish political parties and policies.

Instead "yellow unions" are becoming more popular – cheaper, less political unions. (In Denmark, yellow is the color associated with discounts, while deep blue is associated with high-quality, high-cost products.) I sincerely can't tell you how well these unions represent their members, although you can usually find online ratings. If their services to members aren't good, a union isn't worth joining.

The difference between a union and an *A-kasse*

It took me about a decade to figure out the difference between a Danish union and an *A-kasse*, so I hope I can make the process easier and shorter for you.

As I've explained above, a union gives you information about your industry and protects you on the job, standing in your corner if things go wrong. It also usually negotiates with business owners to set salary levels.

An *A-kasse* distributes your unemployment payments if you have a right to unemployment payments. That usually requires either EU citizenship or a permanent residency card.

In other words, if you've come to Denmark to work from India, China, Africa, the USA, Canada, or any other non-EU area, you usually don't need an *A-kasse* until you are granted permanent residency in Denmark. You can still benefit from a union, however.

If you have permanent residency or are from an EU country, you should sign up for an *A-kasse* as soon as you can. (Some non-EU spouses can also sign up for an *A-kasse*.)

What's an *A-kasse*?

An *A-kasse* is a nonprofit organization that will pay out your *dagpenge*, or unemployment insurance, if you lose your job. It will also usually pay out your *sygedagpenge* – sick leave payments – if you're temporarily too sick to work.

The truth is, the money they distribute comes from the Danish government, and you'll get the same amount no matter which *A-kasse* you choose. The *A-kasse* is just the administrator, which is why you should choose an *A-kasse* with good online reviews for its administrative ability.

Your *A-kasse* will also do various things to try to muscle you back into the workplace, such as helping you update and improve your CV and repeatedly directing you toward job openings. (The Danes have the unsubtle strategy of making unemployment so unpleasant that it's easier to work.)

Skipping an *A-kasse* is a stupid way to save money

You pay for your *A-kasse* on a quarterly basis, but it's deductible from your giant Danish taxes, so it doesn't really cost that much.

Skipping an *A-kasse* is a stupid way to save money. As broke as I occasionally get, I still keep paying for my *A-kasse*, though I've never actually needed to use it.

That's because if you don't have an *A-kasse* and become unemployed or sick, you won't be able to get *dagpenge*. Without *dagpenge*, there's nothing on offer except the dreaded *kontanthjælp* ("cash help"), the payment Denmark offers to the poorest of the poor.

Although the rules change constantly, generally you're not allowed to own anything of value if you accept *kontanthjælp*, which means selling your home, your vehicles, and even your jewelry in some cases. If you have a partner, you may not even be eligible for *kontanthjælp* – the state considers it your partner's job to support you.

It's all very ugly and unpleasant, which is why I suggest signing up for an *A-kasse* as soon as you're eligible. You usually have to be a member for a year before getting any benefits, so sign up while you still have a job.

You can price-shop among *A-kasse* but make sure to do some research on their service levels before just going for the cheapest option.

Make your union work for you

Once you have a union, an *A-kasse*, or both, don't just lean back and send them money without taking advantages of the services they offer, like networking, free courses, and career counseling.

And don't be afraid to switch if you find a better deal. The different unions and *A-kasse* are competitive with each other, and they're constantly coming up with various short-term deals to lure you away from their rivals.

I recently switched myself after someone from a branch of *Lederne*, the manager's union, called up and offered me 24 months' free *lønsikring*. This "income insurance" is a popular product that makes up the often-substantial difference between your actual salary and *dagpenge* if you lose your job.

Talk to your friends and your colleagues about which unions and *A-kasse* they use. If they've got a better one, go ahead and trade up.

There's surprisingly little paperwork involved, and your new *A-kasse* or union will generally take care of it for you. You'll get a sad phone call from the organization you left behind, but other than that it's an easy, painless process.

Job benefits – Your free daily banana

O n-the-job benefits in Denmark come in three categories: the kind every Danish worker gets, the kind everyone at your company gets, and the kind only top dogs at your company get.

When you talk with a future employer, there's not all that much room for negotiation unless you're coming in at a very high level or have a highly sought-after specialty.

In most cases, as American kindergarteners say, "You get what you get, and you don't get upset." Fortunately, job benefits in Denmark tend to be generous.

What everyone gets

Anyone with a full-time job in Denmark is entitled to five weeks' annual paid vacation, in addition to the roughly twelve paid Danish public holidays per year.

If you're on a salary, your employer will also put aside a percentage of your salary as a "vacation allowance" so you can enjoy your time off a bit more. Hourly workers may find themselves covered by *Feriekonto*, the government-run vacation account. (You can read more about time off in Denmark in the chapter *The Danish Art of Taking Time Off.*)

Health coverage in Denmark

Every legal resident in Denmark is also covered by the Danish public health care system – although you should be aware that this insurance is only valid in Denmark. If you live in Denmark and travel to, say, the USA, you'll need to seek out and pay for some extra insurance. (The rules are different for EU citizens, but they still need extra insurance when traveling outside of the EU.)

In addition, every new parent in Denmark is entitled to parental leave. If you're the one birthing the baby, you get to stop working four weeks before the birth (or, if your health requires it, even earlier) and will then receive eleven paid weeks off after the birth, as will the baby's other parent. In addition, you and the other parent will receive 26 weeks to share between you, which can be saved up for later in the child's life if you want. Adoptive parents get similar benefits.

The Danes will think it is strange if you don't take as much leave as possible to spend with your new child.

Topping up your parental leave money

Parental leave is paid for by the government, which gives the parents *barselsdagpenge*, the same amount of money that unemployed people receive. This is probably well under your salary if you've come to Denmark as a professional.

Many companies top up this *barselsdagpenge* so that you receive your full salary during your parental leave. If the company offers this benefit to anyone, they generally offer it to everyone.

The company hot lunch

Another benefit usually offered to everyone at the company is a lunch, usually a hot lunch.

This is a business strategy as much as a benefit: the company doesn't want its people disappearing in the middle of the day to go find a sandwich or order the three-course *prix fixe* in a restaurant. They want them to refuel for 30 minutes and get back to their desks.

Small companies often pay for an external vendor to bring one or two dishes per day that everyone shares. Bigger companies have in-house chefs who produce a huge spread with salads, home-baked bread, and vegetarian options.

These companies often provide breakfast in addition to lunch and sometimes dinners for people who work the late shift. In some places, you can order (and pay for) a pre-packed dinner to take home and share with your family.

There's usually a small monthly charge for the lunch plan, but this is for tax reasons: if you didn't pay for it, it would be taxed as a benefit and end up costing you more.

It's really not a good idea to refuse the lunch plan unless you have specific dietary needs, because not being able to eat with your colleagues cuts you off from the all-important group spirit in Danish workplaces.

If you have religious or medical reasons for avoiding certain foods, the meal providers will usually go out of their way to accommodate you.

Otherwise, bring your food from home and eat it at the same table as your colleagues.

The fruit plan: Your free daily banana

It's also common for Danish workplaces to have a "fruit plan," which provides big bowls of fresh fruit around the office. Each employee is entitled to one piece of fruit per day. Coffee and tea are usually free for employees, and there are sometimes healthy snacks like nuts available to all. Again, this is a business strategy as well as a benefit. Employees who eat nutritious food are less likely to require expensive sick leave.

Surprisingly, health concerns seem to go out the window

when customers come to call. Meetings with external customers are usually catered with sugary sodas, sugary pastries, and sometimes candy in bowls. Go easy on this stuff: I'll never forget the non-Dane who pulled up a bowl of candy and ate the entire thing himself, like a bowl of cereal.

These meeting treats can be worked off at the company gym, which large companies usually provide for all their employees. Smaller companies sometimes subsidize memberships at a local gym.

Pension – public and private

Everyone who works in Denmark must pay into the Danish government pension plan, and most employers also have private plans into which you contribute around 5% of your base salary, and the company contributes an extra 10% of your income. (You can take this money with you if you leave Denmark, although it will be heavily taxed at the time you withdraw it.)

The pension plan usually also includes some extra life insurance and long-term disability insurance. I always choose the plan with the maximum disability coverage available, because the Danish *fortidspension* payments for full disability are difficult to get and not particularly generous.

Why do I need a private health care plan?

Many companies also offer private health care plans to all of their employees and their families. You might ask: "Why do I need a private health care plan in a country like Denmark, where health care is tax-financed and free at the point of care?"

The answer is that public health care doesn't cover

everything. It provides life-saving treatment. Coverage for pain-relieving therapies like acupuncture and reflexology is limited, and so is psychological help or drug counseling if someone in your family should need it.

Your private health plan can cover this type of thing. It also provides quicker access to the kind of non-emergency operation that might require a wait at a public hospital, like a bad knee from a sports injury.

What only the top dogs get

I've described the benefits that everyone in Denmark gets and that everyone at a specific corporation gets.

Now a few words about the benefits you probably won't get unless you're one of the very top dogs at a company or you have a unique skill set.

For example, top executives usually get an extensive bonus or stock option plans, but these are restricted to a certain pay grade. If you're not in that pay grade, it's not something you can negotiate for.

A company car may not be worth it

Company cars are also distributed by pay grade: top executives are usually offered a leased luxury vehicle, although having a driver is considered pompous unless you are a CEO or prime minister. Salespeople may also get a company car if they're expected to travel extensively by road, although they may also be asked to get their own car and then be reimbursed for the mileage.

The problem with getting a leased company car in Denmark is that this is a taxable benefit, and the cost of the taxes may rival the cost of actually owning your own car.

Some companies offer their employees a cash allowance to spend on a car instead, but cash allowances don't accrue pension benefits like your regular salary does.

Bottom line: it might be a good financial move to get the cost of your "free" company car added to your salary and then buy or lease your own car. In that case, however, you'll be responsible for maintenance.

If you live in Copenhagen or Aarhus, you may not need a car at all.

Biking is popular for all ages and economic classes in Denmark. In fact, you'll often see the most aggressive and hungriest Danish executives turn up at the office in Spandex bike racing gear, take a quick shower, and then put on their business suits and conquer the world.

What (almost) nobody gets

A few employee benefits common in other countries are unusual in Denmark.

For example, housing allowances are rare. You'll be expected to pay for your housing on your own, although you may be given a small moving and relocation allowance.

Domestic help is almost never provided, although a few companies will let you pay to drop off your laundry and dry cleaning at the office and have an external company take care of it.

In general, domestic help is rare in Denmark: if you plan to live here, even as a highly-paid professional (and even as a man) you'll need good cooking and cleaning skills.

Wealthy families sometimes have an *au pair* to help with the kids, but generally, you're on your own, with the possible exception of a weekly cleaning person to do the heavy lifting.

If you have children, don't expect a schooling allowance unless you are a very sought-after employee. While there are some excellent international schools in Denmark, you will usually have to pay the tuition yourself.

Putting your child in a Danish school, either a state school or a private one, is smiled upon by the Danes: it is seen as a sign of commitment to Denmark.

Work from home

Working from home is common in Denmark, and many companies will pay for your home internet connection.

They'll also usually pay for a company mobile phone, although this benefit, like so many other Danish benefits, is taxable.

Whenever you're offered a benefit from your Danish employer, it's a good idea to think in terms of – is this taxable, at Danish tax rates?

If it is, your benefit might just cost more than it's worth.

Networking in Denmark – Five useful tips for making Danish business contacts

Networking in Denmark is tough, even for Danes. This is a culture where it's considered a bit shocking to talk to someone you don't know, unless you're drunk, in which case all bets are off.

Denmark is a place where people grow up with their networks. Many Danes still have the same friends they had in primary school, and they develop professional networks through secondary school, university, internship programs, and their first jobs out of school. These are people they know, at least a little bit, so it's okay to talk to them even when sober.

Most jobs in Denmark are found via networks. Somebody mentions on their LinkedIn profile that they're looking for a new team member and the CVs from friends of friends and old classmates start flowing in. And since "social fit" is such an important part of Danish work culture, someone from the network is more likely to seem like a known quantity when it comes to being part of the team.

So, what does this mean to you as an international? It means you're going to have to figure out how to network in Denmark.

Even if you have a job, moving up professionally often requires going to a new company instead of persuading your current company to promote you.

So – how do you build a network?

Tip 1 is to start by getting involved in small groups. If engineers are in the same room as flower arrangers, not a lot of business is going to get done. But I've seen smaller groups that are very effective – for example, native English-speaking women in corporate communications.

Sometimes unions hold networking meetings. A few Danish companies also hold "educational" meetings about the latest developments in their industries. You can often find out about these meetings by following the companies on social media and subscribing to their email newsletters.

Even online seminars are useful, because you'll learn some of the names in your industry and find yourself on mailing lists that could lead to some useful in-person get-togethers.

If there's not a group that's tailored to your professional interests, consider starting one once you're a bit more established, made up of people you'll meet elsewhere in your networking.

Take a course in your field

Tip 2 is to take some kind of course in your field. Not a one-day course, but something that lasts at least two or three months so you can really get to know your classmates.

Look for a course with group work, where you will be forced to talk to each other and create professional relationships. (Don't make the mistake I did and take a course where everyone just stares at their own computers. I took a Photoshop course and didn't know anyone's name by the end, except for the girl who used the course to design fliers for her nude dancing business. We all took an interest in her work.)

So, choose a course where you'll be forced to get to know other people in your field.

In general, it's easier to get a job in Denmark if you have

some kind of Danish educational credentials, which is another thing you can get from a course. Danish employers have often never heard of your university from back home, and they don't know if it's any good. But if you've been rubber-stamped by a Danish institution, even for a short course, that gives them a sense of comfort.

Don't ask for favors; share what you know

Tip 3 is to never try to take more out of your network than you put in.

After a speaking engagement, a man who was new to Denmark came up to me and said he'd met several local people in his industry and was connected to them on LinkedIn. He said, "Now I've asked them for a job three or four times and they don't even write back anymore!"

This guy was going about it all wrong. He was asking from his network without giving back to his network. And that, unfortunately, fits into the nasty stereotype some Danes have about foreigners: that they just come here to take and not give back.

That's silly, and of course you have a lot to share. I think a lot of foreign jobseekers undersell how useful their experience from their home country can be. Denmark is in the forefront of some industries, but it's a small country, and a lot of stuff has already been done well or better elsewhere.

Share what you know; find out what your contact might be interested in and offer that information as part of a meeting. "I see you're putting up a smart building using a specialty HVAC system. I worked extensively with that type of system in my home country. Should we have a quick cup of coffee?"

A quick cup of coffee at their office, kept to a tidy 20 or 30 minutes, is the standard first step for networking with Danes. You'll get a chance to see their company's digs and perhaps even meet their colleagues. Dress as if you were going to a job interview, and be precisely on time for these coffee meetups. Use them to exchange information, not push yourself for a job.

Take care of your network in Denmark

Tip 4 is that once you've begun to build a network, you have to carefully maintain it, a bit like a houseplant. You don't always have the opportunity to meet with your contacts in person, but you can comment on people's online updates and congratulate them on their projects. If there's a job available at your company, post it for your network to share.

And offer support when something goes wrong.

I once left a job very quickly, so I wrote a few brief farewell emails to colleagues I didn't have time to say goodbye to. Most wrote back saying something pleasant and generic – *great working with you, good luck in the future* – but one guy did not.

Let's call him Jeff. Jeff never responded to my email. Later, when I was going for a job at a place where Jeff had worked, I contacted him to see if he had any tips. He never wrote back.

About six months later, I did hear from Jeff. It was a mass email – he had a new product he was selling. He said, *Tell your friends and family about my new product.*

Did I tell my friends and family about his new product? No, I did not.

So, keep your networks warm. It only takes a few words. If someone gets a new job, email them or add a comment on the LinkedIn announcement that's cheerful and upbeat, along the lines of *Congrats, you'll be great!* If someone loses a job you say, *Man, sorry to hear that, I'll keep an eye open for you.* It doesn't take much time, but it means a lot to people.

When Danish people can't remember your name

Tip 5 is to never come to a networking meeting unprepared. You should be following all the major companies in your industry on LinkedIn, so if you meet someone from that company, you can talk intelligently about what's going on there. Their new projects, their new CEO, whatever.

I also recommend having business cards, even though you'll hardly ever use them in Denmark. The one time you need them, it'll be crucial.

Plus, as foreigners, we have to face the fact that it can be hard for Danish people to remember our names. I can't tell you how many times I've been called Kate. *Hey, Kate.* No! That's not my name. (I now say, "*It's Kay – like OK.*")

Someone who finds you interesting may try to connect with you on LinkedIn when he gets home. If he can't quite remember your name – which may be as impenetrable to him as the difference between *Lene Hansen*, *Line Hansen*, and *Lina Hansen* might be to you – you'll never make that connection.

Even if you're not employed yet, make sure the card references something practical that sets you apart from others with similar expertise – say, *Specialist in high-efficiency cooling systems for smart buildings*.

Get nicely-designed cards on quality paper. You never want to have anything that's poorly designed or cheap-looking in Denmark.

Talk to the older people in the room

At a networking meeting, big or small, I always recommend talking to some of the older people in the room. Usually everyone else is trying to talk to the new young hotshot, but older Danish people have a lot of knowledge.

You can ask them, *If you were me, starting out in the industry today, what would you do? Which companies would you want to work for?*

Occasionally you get a Bitter Betty or a Bitter Burt who just wants to talk about how awful the world has become. But generally, older people have more time to talk to you, and they're not always looking over your shoulder to see if there's somebody better across the room.

Bring a conversation starter

If you're a bold person, and you want people to come to you at a networking meeting, carry something large enough to be visible that makes a good conversation opener.

For example, when I go to these things I carry copies of my first book, *How to Live in Denmark,* and sometimes give an autographed copy away to a good business prospect. Other networkers bring tools of their trade, too: I once saw someone looking for maritime work carrying an antique sextant.

Remember, when you're networking, you're not begging. You're offering a business deal as a person who has some useful skills that people need.

You'll know you've succeeded in networking in Denmark when Danes go out of their way to talk to you.

Part 2: Life on the job

Your first day on the job

O n your first day at work in Denmark, you are likely to find a pretty bouquet of flowers on your desk to welcome you.

This terrified a Chinese acquaintance of mine, who was accustomed to receiving flowers on her *last* day at work. She thought she'd been fired before she even sat down.

In Denmark, the bouquet is just a way to say "welcome" and to add some sunshine to an arduous day that is sure to include many handshakes and computer passwords.

Saying hello to your new colleagues

Someone will probably be appointed as your "buddy" on the first day of the job, and that person will take you around to meet the people you'll be working with, as well as showing you practical parts of the office like the printer room and the toilets.

Shake hands with everyone you meet and try to remember their first names – although you'll probably get a lot of duplicates. (Depending on the size of the company, you can expect to meet at least two or three people named Mette, Søren, Pia, Rasmus, or Lars.)

Last names aren't important, at least until you have to find these people on an email list. "Mr." and "Ms.", or their Danish equivalents "*Hr.*" and "*Fru*," are almost never used in Denmark.

Don't act overly impressed when you meet the top bosses: this will embarrass them.

The people you really need to be deferential to are the administrative staff.

Be kind to the administrators

If you come from a country with a large population and a great deal of unemployment, you may be accustomed to a large staff of secretaries who help you with filling out forms, tracking expenses, setting up meetings, and other small tasks.

Such helpful people are rare in Denmark, where most professionals are expected to do these things themselves using online tools.

Often an entire department will be expected to make do with one administrative assistant, who officially reports to the top dog.

This administrator might be able to help you with the online tools once or twice – but only to teach you how to use them yourself.

Treat these administrative people with the extreme respect they deserve. You'll need their help now, with all the complications of getting started on the job, and you'll need them sometime in the future when you least expect it.

Also, be kind to employees who help with coffee or other refreshments. A hospital head-of-staff once told me about a foreign doctor who began his tenure by being rude and dismissive to the coffee lady. He soon found himself as the only man in a meeting with no coffee.

Tidying up your desk, cleanup after team breakfasts

Sloppiness is not considered charming in Denmark, which is located just north of order-loving Germany.

You'll be expected to leave your desk tidy at the end of your first workday and any other workday, and to remove any leftover food or drinks. Many companies also expect you to wash out your coffee or teacup or to place it in the shared dishwasher.

Some teams eat Friday breakfasts together, and staff take turns putting away the bread and cheese and juice afterwards.

It may seem a little odd, as a trained professional, to occasionally be doing the work of a kitchen lady. But this is how the Danes do it, and they won't be pleased if you suggest it's beneath you.

Full-time cleaning staff take care of sweeping floors and other larger tasks. It's considered good manners in Denmark to greet them when you see them and even chat a bit.

One employee from India told me that he was shocked to see his department head sharing a joke with the cleaner. That would never happen in his country, he said.

It happens in Denmark because it's considered good style for the boss to show that she sees herself as the equal of everyone else on the team, no more or less important than the cleaner.

Actually, if the boss was away for a few days, business would probably run as usual. If the cleaner didn't show up, the result would be chaos.

Leaving the office – when to do it, when not to do it

Generally, you don't leave your Danish workplace during the workday unless you have a very good reason, such as a client meeting, or if you or your child suddenly become ill.

Lunch out is unusual in most companies – the team eats together in the company canteen – and leaving the office for personal errands is frowned upon.

If you need to see a doctor on a workday, try to schedule it very early or very late in the day so you don't miss much work. If that's not possible, or if you need the entire afternoon for a particularly grueling dentist appointment, it's usually okay to take time off work.

Try not to schedule meetings later than 3pm or so. Your colleagues (male and female) who have young children will begin leaving about this time to make the pickup from day-care.

These loving parents will either end up missing the meeting or get annoyed at having to move their schedules around in order to attend.

Don't say "go' morgen" after 10am

Greeting your colleagues when you arrive and saying goodbye when you leave is always good practice, particularly if you work in an open-plan office.

That said, the expression *go' morgen* in Danish doesn't correspond directly to "good morning" in English.

While "good morning" can be said until 11:59am in most English-speaking countries, followed by "good afternoon" and "good evening," the time limit on the Danish *go' morgen* runs out at about 10am.

Saying *go' morgen* after that time has a slightly sarcastic tone, along the lines of "Well, it took you awhile to get here. Thanks for showing up."

The correct greeting after 10am is *go' dag* (good day) followed by *go' aften* (good evening) at around 5pm. *Go' nat*, or good night, is only said when someone is getting ready to put on their pajamas.

Understanding your Danish boss

D anish bosses don't like to flaunt their authority. The social cues that point to a big cheese in other cultures – the flashy watch, the big office, the glamorous yet servile executive assistant – are considered poor taste in egalitarian Denmark.

So are the booming, take-charge personalities many foreigners may expect from a boss.

Denmark is a flat country. It is flat geographically, you are expected to keep a flat temperament and vocal tone, and (as they love to tell you) Danish companies have a relatively flat management structure.

This means fewer layers of people to keep an eye on you, which can be a refreshing thing, but also fewer people around to help if you're confused or overwhelmed.

Less like a general, more like a sports coach

Trying to figure out their Danish boss can be difficult for foreigners. If your culture is full of strong leaders who drive their teams forward like a general leading troops into battle, you may find your Danish boss passive and even difficult to respect.

A Danish boss is less like an army general and more like a sports coach. She outlines how important it is to win the game, brings in people she believes have the right qualifications, and gives them the outline of what she wants done.

Then she sets them loose on the playing field to go do their jobs.

The secret lunchtime meeting

Not trusting employees to get the work done on their own is seen as an insult.

I saw an example of this at one of my first corporate jobs in Denmark, where I worked as a Danish-English translator at a large bank. One day our department head asked us to kindly let her know when we were going to lunch and when we returned, so she could allocate resources and make sure there was coverage for urgent assignments.

This seemed reasonable to me, but my fellow translators were furious: they held a secret lunchtime meeting to discuss what they saw as an outrageous suggestion. They were not schoolchildren or factory workers, they told each other in the company canteen. They were professionals, and as long as they got their work done promptly and correctly, there was no reason to monitor when they were in the office and when they weren't.

The boss backed down. In Denmark, the workers' needs are often given more consideration than the customers' needs. Any urgent translations would have to wait until the translators got back from lunch – or the boss could do them herself.

Danish bosses don't monitor your time in the office

In general, your Danish boss won't monitor how much time you spend in the office. In fact, if you spend too much time there, she may worry that you can't handle your job.

Apart from special peak periods, the general Danish attitude is that any job worth doing should be doable in the official workweek of 37 hours. There are no real prizes for working beyond that.

That said, when you are at work, you're expected to fully focus on the job and to deliver exactly what you said you would deliver at precisely the time you promised to deliver it.

Delays and excuses are toxic in Danish business life, particularly when they arrive at the last minute. They wreak havoc with the quality and competence every Danish company likes to project.

If you're having trouble with an assignment and don't think you'll be able to deliver on time, let your boss know as soon as problems begin to arise. That way she can make plans to get you some backup or move around deadlines.

Revealing at the last minute that an assignment won't be ready on time is a recipe for a very angry Danish boss.

When your Danish boss is angry

Anger is a slightly forbidden emotion in Denmark. Like sexuality in conservative countries, it is expected to be expressed in private.

That means if your boss is angry at you, she will probably call you to a conference room and have a chat with you one-on-one. ("Hanging someone out" in front of others – or pointing out their failings while others watch – is considered extremely bad manners in Denmark. Make sure not to do it yourself when someone else on your team drops the ball.)

At any rate, the one-on-one chat with your boss is where things can go wrong.

She will be trying to express an uncomfortable emotion (anger) in a second language (English). The wording can often come out as harsh and even rude.

Anyway, confrontations like these are when many foreigners decide they don't like their Danish bosses, or that their Danish bosses are stubborn and inflexible.

Keep in mind that it's difficult for Danes to reprimand people, because it makes it all too clear that they are not equal. It makes the boss an authority figure, and this is an anti-authoritarian culture.

So, spare a little sympathy for your Danish boss's awkward situation and embarrassment at having to be the higher-up and bad guy. If you did fail to live up to expectations, admit that and work toward a solution. Even better, proactively point out your own mistakes, which will make the boss feel she can trust you.

When your Danish boss is happy

Since doing your job well is the presumed default in Danish companies, your boss may not say all that much when he is happy with your work. Celebrating success is not a core skill in Denmark.

This can be disconcerting for foreigners, particularly Americans, who are raised on constant applause aimed at boosting their self-esteem. More than one American has told me that they thought they were on the verge of being fired before an annual employee review confirmed that they were, in fact, doing an excellent job.

You, too, may not get any indication you're doing well until the formal yearly evaluation – standard in most corporate jobs – when your boss may applaud your wonderful performance.

In the meantime, no news is generally good news. If you feel you need feedback or have something on your mind, most Danish bosses have an open-door policy. You can just drop in to his office for a chat or schedule 15 minutes at the end of the day to talk about how you're doing.

There's not much reason to be afraid of the boss in Denmark. He will often have his desk next to you in an open-plan office, not hidden behind glass and a forbidding secretary. He'll eat lunch with you in the company canteen, share a beer with the staff after work on Friday, or even boogie down with you at the company Christmas party.

Your boss wants to see himself as part of the team. Clearly, he's that part of the team that organizes and supervises and evaluates and takes responsibility for the biggest decisions, but still just part of the team.

Equal, just like everyone else.

Handling a meeting in Denmark

D anish business meetings can be brisk and efficient, or they can be extraordinarily long, as the people attending seek consensus on whatever issue they need to discuss. There's an old Danish saying that "A disagreement is a discussion that ended too soon."

So, get to the meeting location precisely on time – or even a couple of minutes early – and be ready for the long haul.

One thing that sets apart Danish (or Nordic) meetings is that every single person, from the boss down to the student helper, will be having his or her say on the matter at hand.

There is no particular hierarchy or order in a meeting, often no written agenda, and no requirement that any one particular person speaks first or speaks last.

The only thing that's a "must" is that you're well-enough researched in your part of the meeting to have an intelligent opinion, and that you express it directly and politely.

Well-considered and even provocative questions are okay too, as long as they relate to the topic at hand.

You are expected to challenge the boss

One of the most difficult things for people from hierarchical cultures to learn is that it's perfectly okay to disagree with your Danish boss at these meetings, assuming you do so respectfully and have facts to back up your point of view.

In fact, your bosses will probably be angrier if you act like a yes-man and fail to point out obvious flaws in their arguments that might lead to a disastrous business decision. ("*Why didn't you say anything?*")

Danish children are brought up to challenge their parents and teachers. In this anti-authoritarian culture, silent obedience buys you nothing.

Do Danish meetings have any purpose?

Whatever gets decided at the meeting may be reversed the next day if someone gets a better idea or if new information comes in.

In fact, you may leave the meeting feeling you've accomplished nothing at all. But you have: you've been part of the consensus.

What to wear to work in Denmark

There's no reason to spend a lot on your Danish business wardrobe. Danes, by nature, are not flashy dressers.

In most Danish business environments, you'll be perfectly well dressed in a pair of business trousers, dark shoes, and a solid-color sweater or dress shirt. Male or female, you'll never go wrong with quiet colors like burgundy, dark blue, dark green, brown, or black.

Subtle good taste is the preferred style. Obvious designer labels are considered tacky, but quality cut and fabric are appreciated.

Suits and ties are only required in the financial industry, although younger bankers often prefer an open collar. Some salespeople also wear business suits to make their products look more high-end.

In casual environments like the gaming industry, hoodies are common.

The executive uniform for men and women

The standard uniform for Danish male executives is a blue business suit, a pale shirt open at the collar, and leather shoes.

Female executives wear pretty but modest blouses or expensive knits with expensive accessories. Women are almost never required to wear a dress in Denmark unless they are meeting with Danish royalty, and even then, many women wear formal trouser suits.

High heels, fancy hairstyles are impractical

If you like wearing dresses and skirts, you can, although the Danish love of bicycling means that skirts worn in Denmark are generally long and loose.

Women who wear short skirts usually wear thick hose or leggings or even trousers beneath them. This is less about modesty and more about warmth.

High heels are uncommon in Denmark: any shoes that are difficult to walk in are considered *upraktisk* (impractical) and anathema to the sensible Danes. Heels are particularly treacherous on uneven bricks or cobblestones, which you'll still find on many Danish streets.

Danish women's make-up is generally light and natural-looking, and their hairstyles simple.

This is at least in part because Denmark is a windy, rainy country: the exquisitely painted face or complex hairstyle you leave home with is unlikely to make it to your destination.

Spend your money on outerwear

A good investment in work clothing is a high-end coat or jacket to wear during Denmark's long winter, which lasts from roughly October to April.

You'll be arriving to meet business contacts and shaking hands while still wearing your coat, so your military surplus duffle jacket from your college days is probably not the best choice.

Cashmere coats are not required, but well-made, waterproof outerwear that won't crush your business clothes will be worth its weight in gold.

Keep in mind that while Denmark is chilly in winter, it is rarely Arctic. Some foreigners arrive with fleece-lined parkas more suitable for northern Norway than for Denmark. They sweat their way through a few October afternoons before realizing they've made the wrong choice.

Buy your wardrobe when you get to Denmark

You can also buy your outerwear after you get to Denmark. There's a wide selection, and it's often discounted, meaning it only costs twice as much as it would anywhere else instead of three or four times as much.

In fact, buying the majority of your Danish work wardrobe after you get to Denmark isn't a bad idea. After a couple of months on the job, you'll get a sense of what the general "look" is in your company or industry.

To get your Danish-conforming wardrobe, shop the semi-annual sales at the local department stores – it's what the Danes do. You can also order online, but always buy from shops that ship from within the European Union to avoid punishing customs fees.

Is learning to speak Danish worth it?

In one of my seminars, I met an Irishman who had fallen in love with a Danish woman.

He agreed to move to Denmark and thought it would be better for his job prospects if he learned to speak Danish.

"Why not just learn Norwegian? It's easier," his girlfriend said cheerfully.

Spoken Danish can be a headache

The poor man did start to learn Norwegian, only to be told by his laughing girlfriend that her suggestion was an example of the famous Danish humor.

But she was correct that Norwegian is probably easier to pick up. Danish is a difficult language to learn, even if you speak its close linguistic cousins, English and German.

While the written language isn't too tough to figure out, the spoken language is a headache. Danes pronounce only small bits of each word and smash those small bits together.

One foreigner told me the story of two boys he saw trading football cards on a train. "*Davilik!*" "*Davilik!*" the boys kept crying out.

The foreigner, who was working hard to learn Danish, tried to look up *Davilik* in his dictionary – without success. There was no such word.

It was only months later that he realized they were saying, "*Det vil jeg ikke!*" or "I don't want to make that trade."

Even the Swedes and Norwegians have trouble understanding spoken Danish.

"May I push you?" and more useful phrases

If you're only in Denmark for a few months, it might not be worth the investment in time to learn much more than the basic pleasantries in Danish.

Tak for "thank you" is good to know, and so is *undskyld* for "excuse me" when you bump into someone. (The Danes don't always say *undskyld* themselves – they just charge right ahead or say *Må jeg skub' lidt?*, which translates to "May I push you?" But it's a good word to know nonetheless.)

Tak for nu, "thanks for now," is a good way to thank people for giving you a bit of their time; the next time you see them, you can say, *Tak for sidst*, or "thanks for the last time we were together."

English as a corporate language

You may have been recruited by a company that has English as its corporate language. Technically, this means that all meetings must be held in English, and emails and company documents are supposed to be in English too.

This is easier said than done, but at least that's the official policy.

What often happens in companies that choose English as a corporate language is that they become a house divided.

Foreigners and young Danes who speak English well are on one side, and older Danes who struggle with English are on the other.

Danes who struggle with English

As a foreigner, you may sense a mild resentment from these older Danes. They have a point – the English requirement was probably imposed after they were long into their careers. It can be embarrassing for someone who is a technical expert in his or her own language to have to stumble through a meeting in English because you have joined the team.

If they seem uncomfortable around you, that's probably why. Please try not to take this personally.

Danes who struggle with English are actually a gift to you, because when you do begin to learn Danish, they'll be happy to let you practice with them. (It's a perennial complaint of foreigners that Danes switch to English whenever they hear a foreign accent.)

Learning Danish means more job opportunities

If you plan to stay in Denmark for more than a year or so, it's a good idea to learn some Danish – and your visa may require that you do so.

Even if you're not forced to, it's a good idea to learn Danish if you plan to make a commitment to Denmark. It'll make daily life easier: you'll stop wanting to tear your hair out every time you run across a website or voicemail that's only available in Danish.

You'll have more job opportunities, since around half of the positions in Denmark are with national, regional, or local governments. Almost all governmental jobs require a working knowledge of Danish.

Plus, a lot of social life in Denmark takes place in Danish; Danes, understandably, want to speak Danish to each other, particularly when they're off duty with a beer in hand.

My experience when I first arrived was that they'd kindly speak English while I was there, but as soon as I took a moment away to take a phone call or order another round, the conversation switched to Danish.

When I returned, it continued in Danish for a while until I interrupted, or until some kind person grudgingly returned the conversation to English.

Learning Danish makes you a full part of Danish society. You'll be able to follow the behind-the-scenes maneuvers at the office more closely and join in on the usual lunchtime discussions about Danish politics and Danish TV.

If you have children or plan to have children, you'll be able to communicate with their Danish-speaking playmates from the daycare center.

Not having to rush to Google Translate to find out how to say, "Stop hitting the dog!" in Danish can be worth the long hours of study on its own.

Places to practice speaking Danish

The first friendships or acquaintanceships you make with Danish friends will probably be in English. In most cases, relationships that start in English continue in English.

So, if you want to practice your Danish, you'll probably need to form friendships with new Danes, or join groups where Danish is the *lingua franca*. Running clubs, knitting clubs, building association boards, and political groups are all good options.

Another tip I offer to foreigners who want to practice their Danish is to seek out the "Elderlearn" programs run by many municipalities.

These organizations will arrange ongoing visits with a sweet but lonely older person who will be pleased to chat with you in Danish for as long as you like.

The secrets of socializing with your Danish colleagues

When you work in a Danish office, you'll often find yourself invited to impromptu in-office social events with your Danish colleagues. Somebody has a birthday, someone's having a baby, somebody has been with the company for ten years, someone is going on vacation the next day. And they almost all involve cake.

Cake is very important in Denmark. Cake builds bridges. Cake makes friends. And when there's cake on offer, as a foreigner, it's a good idea to show up and accept it.

When I first started working in a Danish office, I made a big mistake. I said no to cake.

It's important to show up for the cake

I would think – *No, I have work to do at my desk. I have to finish this report.* Or else, *I'm eating healthy! It's swimsuit season.* So, I wouldn't take a break. I wouldn't eat the cake.

That was wrong. That was poor cake etiquette. In-office socializing is the way to get to know your Danish colleagues, because you probably won't hang out with your colleagues much outside of work. This is your big chance to chat about things not directly related to the job at hand. It's all about the cake.

Even if you really can't eat cake for some reason, show up, get a cup of coffee or tea and chat for ten minutes. Congratulate the cake-giver on whatever the occasion might be. This makes you seem like part of the team, part of the group.

The fact is, Danish companies often have a big problem with the silo effect – one colleague doesn't know what the other is working on. A cake break is a chance to casually find out what that guy across the room actually does all day.

"Private friends"

It's good to get to know your colleagues – they can be one of the highlights of working in Denmark. I've had some great colleagues over the years, really wonderful people. It's a great way to get to know Danes, practice speaking Danish, and learn about Danish culture.

But you should not expect your Danish colleagues to become friends outside the office or "private friends," as the term is sometimes translated directly from Danish (*private venner*).

You should not even expect to see them outside the office. In other countries – Germany, England, Japan – people often get together with their colleagues outside the office, go out and drink a beer, or play golf.

This is unusual in Denmark if you're over 30, or even younger if your workmates are already married with children. Danes like to spend their time with their established friends and family networks.

Time outside of work is family time, time off. When you say goodbye to your colleagues on Friday afternoon, you probably won't have any contact with them until Monday morning.

Heavy drinking at the staff party

There are a few exceptions. If you like to run, someone will be eager to sign you up for the company running team or external running events at which your company competes with other companies. Some companies also have competitive bicycling teams, which have largely replaced golf as the best way to socialize with the powerbrokers.

Many companies have a staff party (to which spouses and partners are not invited) once or twice a year, usually one around Christmas and one in the summer. I hated these things, because I'm not a party animal and I don't drink much alcohol. But I recommend going anyway, just to show you're part of the group.

If you don't drink alcohol at all, pour yourself a soda and hang out at the party with the people who have to drive home. They can't drink alcohol either.

After a certain point in the evening, usually around 9pm or so, everyone is so drunk that no one really notices whether you are there or not. You can make your excuses and quietly slip out. As long as you've shown your face, you've demonstrated that you're part of the group.

Your boss is also likely to show up at these parties and may make a fool of herself after too much alcohol. The Danish way is to come to work the next day, say *Tak for sidst*, and otherwise pretend as if nothing embarrassing happened.

Eating lunch with your colleagues

At some companies, the entire staff eats lunch together, or at least the entire department. Usually around noon someone will walk through the work area and say, *Vi spiser!* which translates to "We're eating!" You're expected to put down your work and join the team for lunch.

In a big company, this will usually be in the company canteen. You pay a monthly fee to eat there (usually not very much, just enough to avoid it being taxed as a benefit) and the food is generally good. When I first arrived in Denmark, the dishes were almost always traditional Danish food – lots of pork – but these days there are a lot more diverse options.

Smaller companies often have a van drive up and deliver one meal per day for everyone to eat. This can be good for a while, but it can get repetitive, because the vendors that provide the food usually get into a groove and stay there. One of the companies I worked for had a vendor that made stir-fried dishes, and I think I ate stir-fried food every day for three months. It was a bit much.

Anyway, I sometimes found it difficult to eat lunch with my colleagues. When it's time for me to take a break from work, I like to relax and clear out my mind, maybe respond to personal emails and texts, or just be quiet for a while.

But that's not really what's expected in a Danish office – it can mark you as someone who's not really part of the team. My compromise was to eat with colleagues two or three times a week. That seemed to be enough.

Friday morning bread, Friday evening bar

Some offices also share bread and coffee for an hour or so on Friday, with everyone taking a turn to stop by the bakery and purchase the buns. There are often departmental announcements at these *morgenbrød* sessions, so there's no way to avoid them.

Around 3pm on Friday, someone at the company will uncork a bottle of wine and put out a few beers for the team. This is *fredagsbar*, or Friday bar. It's less likely to include business content, but it's still a good way to socialize with your colleagues.

Don't eat the very last piece of cake

Back to the cake. At some point, it will be your turn to bring cake for your colleagues – maybe it's your birthday, or you're going on vacation. It's okay to buy your cake at one of the excellent bakeries in Denmark. You don't get extra points for a homemade cake.

As a matter of fact, while some Danish homemade cakes are excellent – like Dream Cake (*drømmekage*) with brown sugar and coconut topping – some are awful. Homemade chocolate cake in Denmark tends to taste like a cardboard box. So feel free to buy your cake instead of baking it yourself. No one will think any less of you.

There's one more rule you should know about eating cake in Denmark, which is that it's considered rude to eat the last piece – at least without asking everyone else first if they would like to eat it. But that's not always possible if, say, the last bits of a cake are sitting in the communal kitchen.

This happened to me once when I worked at Carlsberg. After everyone had eaten a slice of a wonderful birthday cake, there was one last piece on the kitchen counter.

Of course, no one wanted to take the last piece, so the first person with a sweet tooth sliced the piece in half.

And then the next person sliced that half in half.

And again, and again, so all that was left was a thin little slice that was almost transparent.

But hey – nobody had taken the last piece. They were all good colleagues who knew their cake etiquette.

Danish humor: Sarcasm, Failure Cake, and "Big Arm Movements"

Having a sense of humor about yourself – what the Danes call "self-irony" – is one of the most important elements of fitting into Danish society and the Danish workplace.

This can take a while to get used to for foreigners from countries where hierarchy, honor, or "face" is important.

In Denmark, if you drop the ball at work, drop your lunch entrée down the front of your business shirt, or make a fool of yourself for any other reason, you're supposed to be able to laugh at your own bumbling.

In fact, the Danes have a tradition called the *kvajebajer* (failure beer) or *kvajekage* (failure cake.)

The person who makes a big mistake offers this beer or cake to others as a way of playfully admitting that he or she failed to live up to expectations.

One of my LinkedIn contacts, for example, worked for a small company that failed to meet an important delivery date by two days. When the company founders finally delivered the product, they also delivered a brightly-colored "failure cake," which everyone took a few moments out of the workday to enjoy.

Not all Danish humor is funny

Making fun of yourself can be fun and light-hearted, but Danish humor is not always so gentle.

When directed at others, Danish humor is a perennial source of confusion for foreigners, and it can be a source of misunderstanding and discomfort in the office.

The basis of Danish humor is keeping people's egos in line by cutting down anyone who thinks himself better than others. At its best, it's good-natured and playful, but it can also be dry, dark, and weird, and occasionally passive-aggressive and cruel. It is rarely laugh-out-loud funny.

For example, I was in a meeting held at one of the renovated 18th-century buildings beloved by the Danish creative class. We were upstairs in a room that had been converted from an attic. Thick wooden beams held up the slanting walls.

One of the meeting participants reached down to plug in her computer and, sitting up too quickly, bashed her head against the thick beam.

There was a loud "thunk" as her skull hit the heavy wood and an uncomfortable moment as she clutched her aching head.

Then someone in the room broke the silence. "No damage done," he said cheerfully. "Not much in there anyway."

She was Danish – she thought it was funny. Someone else might not have.

Danes see sarcasm as a sign of intelligence

For Danes, biting sarcasm is seen as proof of intelligence, confidence, and wit. Foreigners already dealing with cultural confusion don't always see it that way, particularly if the sarcasm is coming from their supervisor.

Most Danes are smart enough to avoid the worst aspects of Danish humor with newcomers, but sometimes a little barbed comment slips out anyway.

For example, if you arrive at a meeting a few minutes late, the meeting leader might say drily, "Nice watch you've got there. Does it work?" That's a joke – and a reminder that tardiness is not appreciated.

It's often said that when a foreigner is included into a circle of Danish humor, it's because Danes know they can take it and that they have accepted you as part of the group.

Until then, remember that if a Dane seems to be making fun of you, they are trying to laugh *with* you, not at you.

Or they are trying to get you to fall in line. It's hard to be sure.

Danes don't laugh at the end of their jokes or say "just kidding." Instead, they sit there stone-faced, waiting for you to respond with a biting quip of your own.

If you're not sure if what someone is saying is supposed to be a joke, ask them.

Don't make "big arm movements"

While passive aggression is common in Denmark, open warfare is not.

Don't raise your voice. Don't yell. Don't send angry emails. Don't wave your arms around to make a point. (The Danes have a saying for people they see as too expressive – "he has big arm movements.") And never, ever lose your temper.

In many cultures, losing your temper is seen as a sign of power and passion. Making a scene is a way of showing that you really care about something. If that something is an important personal relationship or an honorable political position, losing your temper is seen as noble and justified.

This is not true in Danish culture, where losing your temper is seen as a sign that you are childish, unable to control yourself, and basically untrustworthy.

Danes immediately lose respect for someone who "melts

down." If you think you're going to blow your top at work, excuse yourself and go take a walk. (I've done it myself a few times.)

Someone who has been on the receiving end of your anger won't forget quickly and won't be afraid to tell his friends or business contacts about your "crazy" behavior.

You never want to have an enemy in a small country like Denmark, where you will meet the same people again and again.

Working together online

Distance working has become common in Denmark. The Danish colleague on the other end of your virtual meeting might be at home, at their rural summer house, or on a vacation getaway in Spain instead of in the office.

Be on time — or early, to avoid technical difficulties

When you're meeting virtually, all the usual rules about working with Danes are amplified.

Be there on time, or even a bit early, to get any technical difficulties worked out. Make sure you contribute to every conversation, even those with the corporate layers above you, something which can be a bit scary for people from more hierarchical cultures.

If you have a chance to help plan the virtual meeting, see if you can arrange for breakout rooms, where more will get done than in a massive online crowd.

Background more important than wardrobe

How you look during a virtual meeting is not particularly important, as long as you're decently covered. It's not unusual to see the Danish big boss in a hoodie during a virtual call.

However, do try to arrange for either a neutral background – bookshelf or the like – or blur whatever is behind you.

I recently had a distracting online meeting with a good-looking fellow who had chosen to hold a dull discussion of accounting practices in front of a giant double bed in his bedroom.

Danish directness is amplified

One tricky aspect of working virtually with Danes is that their usual sarcasm and directness is even more noticeable.

Video calls at least have the benefit of a face and a smile, but emails, chats, and audio calls with Danes can come off as short, sharp, and almost condescending.

They aren't meant that way: Danes just don't like small talk and do it only under protest.

"Just no"

One American executive told me about an online chat she had with her Danish counterpart about an upcoming project. She proposed getting their two teams together to build relationships before the project began.

"No," the Danish executive responded, followed by silence.

Just "*no*"? the American executive wondered. Not, "Let's discuss it" or "I'm not sure"?"

"I think it would be a waste of time," the Dane volunteered.

Directness as a form of elegance

Danish directness, for them, is a form of elegance.

Why slow things down with a bunch of puffy words that are not needed? Better to save time and get on with business.

But from a distance, this can be as bracing as a cold Nordic wind.

Don't work on other people's schedules

If you're working in a different time zone than your Danish colleagues, you may find yourself getting emails or other work communication at a time when they're at work and you are not.

In most cases, they won't expect an immediate answer. (One big company I work with has a standard signature on every email that says, "*My working hours may not be the same as yours. Please don't feel compelled to respond to me outside of your working hours.*")

Your own working culture may prioritize 24-hour availability, but Danes do not. In a country where money and status are less important than they are in many other places, free time is more valuable than gold.

The flip side, of course, is if you urgently need your Danish colleague to answer a question or approve a decision, they may not be available when you need them.

This can be the case on evenings, weekends, or even during the long, relaxing three or four-week summer vacations Danes look forward to all year.

Birthdays and gifts in the Danish workplace

B irthdays are a big deal in Denmark. When your birthday comes around, you may arrive in the morning to find that your colleagues have planted a Danish flag on your desk, or even decorated your desk with a string of tiny Danish flags.

This isn't a nationalist statement, just a general statement of birthday joy. (I once tried adding my own national flag to the birthday arrangement, which seemed to confuse them.)

Your colleagues may also compliment you on the day's weather. Good behavior over the previous year is thought to result in a sunny birthday.

You bring the cake on your birthday

When it's your birthday, it's your job to bring a cake or cookies to share with the team. No need to overthink this and bring something special from your home country: what your colleagues really want is the type of cake they know best. A "cake person" from the local bakery is a popular choice. You can have them decorate it with frosting that spells out your name or illustrates some distinguishing characteristic, like a stethoscope for a doctor.

Gifts are generally not given, unless you are celebrating a "round" birthday like 30, 40, 50, or 60. In that case, someone in the office may take up a collection for a joint gift, or the office petty cash may be opened to purchase a nice Danish design vase or a coffee table book full of lovely pictures. (Most Danish gifts include "gift stickers" which allow you to quietly exchange them for something you like better.)

At Christmas time, the company sometimes gives a holiday gift to employees. It's usually a small luxury item. Either everyone gets the same thing or you are allowed to choose from several options of equal value. Generally that value will be carefully chosen so that you do not have to pay taxes the gift you receive.

If a client offers you a gift

Denmark is regularly listed among the least corrupt countries in the world, which is one of it its charms. Many Danish companies have policies against accepting gifts from clients. This is both for ethical reasons and because they see it as unfair to colleagues who don't get to meet clients and don't get any presents.

Ask your boss about this. Some companies require that all client gifts be turned in to HR to be shared at the company Christmas party. Others have exceptions for gifts of modest value, which allows you to accept small items like a T-shirt with the client's logo.

"Experience" gifts, such as an invitation to a nice restaurant at the client's expense, should also be disclosed to your boss. There are sometimes specific limits on the price of a dinner you may accept, or even the price of a bottle of wine you can uncork at the table.

Gifts to your colleagues aren't necessary

It's not necessary to give your Danish boss a gift at any time – in fact, it would probably make your boss uncomfortable. Nor do you need to give gifts to any of your colleagues except on very special occasions, such as a new baby in the house.

In this case, some energetic person from the office will probably circulate and collect money from everyone to contribute to a team present.

If you know the person being celebrated, a contribution of DK50 is a nice gesture, but don't be afraid to say "no." A card may be circulated for signatures as well. You generally don't sign the card unless you've chipped in for the present.

Decoding your Danish pay slip and your Danish taxes

Many internationals in Denmark take advantage of a special tax plan for researchers and other highly-educated or highly-paid people. This allows them to pay a reduced income tax of 27% for up to seven years.

If you're not lucky enough to arrive in Denmark under that program (I wasn't), you'll pay the same ambitious income tax rates the Danes pay in order to finance Denmark's generous social welfare services.

A-tax vs B-tax

Danish income taxes can be confusing, however, because they are divided into so many different parts.

Your main job is subject to "*A-skat*" or A-tax; if you do outside work like speaking engagements or catering on the weekends, that will come under the category of "*B-skat*" or B-tax.

(Double-check that your visa allows for outside work; some non-EU internationals have been sent home for taking on very minor extra jobs.)

Brutto vs Netto

The most important two lines on the pay slip are *brutto*, which is what your employer is paying you, and *netto*, which is what you'll actually get to take home.

In between will be several lines of taxes you must pay.

The national government levies a labor market contribution called the *AM-bidrag*, as well as *bundskat* (bottom tax) and, if you earn a comfortable income, a *topskat* (top tax). (There used to be a "middle tax," too, but this was abolished a few years ago.)

Then your municipality, or *kommune*, levies its own *kommuneskat*. Different municipalities have different tax levels: in Copenhagen, for example, the independent municipality of Frederiksberg is well-known for having lower *kommuneskat* than the city around it.

You may also notice a small church tax (*kirkeskat*), which goes to support the Danish state church and its pretty buildings.

If you're not a Christian and don't want to pay the church tax, you can go to the church office for your *sogn* (diocese) and sign a statement saying you are not a believer. Note that nonbelievers cannot be married in a Danish state church (unless they marry a believer) and will not receive a funeral blessing if they are so unfortunate as to die in Denmark.

Some helpful deductions from income taxes

A few items are deducted from your income before tax is assessed. You get a basic personal deduction (*personfradrag*), and your union fees and *A-kasse* contributions are deducted too.

Much of this will be done automatically for you, since the unions send membership information directly to the tax authorities. When you receive your tax assessment notice, the deductions will already have been made.

Other deductions you may have to enter yourself. While interest payments on loans from Danish banks are automatically deducted, interest payments to foreign banks may not be.

Transport costs for people who have a long trip to work or need to work away from home can also be deductible. You might need help from your HR department or an accountant to properly calculate these deductions.

Don't forget that Danish taxes are supposed to be paid on your income from anywhere in the world, not just your income in Denmark.

Indirect taxes

In addition to direct taxes on your income, there are plenty of indirect taxes in Denmark, too. The one you'll pay nearly every day is *MOMS*, which is a sales tax or value-added tax of 25% that has already been added to the price of most items. (A few things, like postage, are exempt from *MOMS*.)

You'll also be paying "green taxes" on your electricity and water bills, plus tax on fuel if you drive a car. Purchasing a new car means a tax of up to 150% on luxury models, which is why the first thing Danes often do when they move outside the country is buy a really fancy car.

If your income changes, tell the tax people

At the end of each year, the tax department will send you a *forskudsopgørelse* (preliminary tax estimate), an outline of how much money they expect you to earn in the year ahead, and how much taxes you will pay each month.

If you earn more than that, you'll be liable for extra taxes; if you earn less, you'll get some cash back after the tax year is over.

Should you suddenly find yourself earning a lot more money, it's a good idea to increase your monthly payment. Otherwise, the bill at the end of the year could be ugly.

You can change your monthly tax payments online and ask questions that will be answered by a friendly tax employee.

As demanding as the Danish tax system can be, it's relatively well-run and easy to navigate. All the calculations are done for your automatically. Your only job will be to look them through, and they are usually correct.

Don't cheat on your taxes. In Denmark, paying your "fair share" of social welfare costs is the closest thing to a contemporary national religion.

Don't work when you're sick, plus dealing with stress

In some countries, "working sick" is a badge of honor. You are supposed to be so dedicated to your team or to the assignment that you come to work even if you feel awful.

In Denmark, the opposite is true. If you feel you've got the beginnings of something that could be contagious, you are considered a better team member if you stay home that day and care for your health. You are not expected to work from home or answer emails if you are ill.

It's also considered okay to take a day or two off if you have a sick child at home, although in these cases, you may be asked to participate in an online meeting or some other work-related activity while your little darling sleeps.

One thing that's *not* considered okay is to call in sick when you really just want a day off for some other reason. (In that case, you should ask for a "personal day," which generally comes out of your annual vacation allotment.)

Danish workplaces are built on trust. If it comes out that you were not actually ill but said you were, that breakdown in trust could be the first step towards a termination.

Maybe you know in advance that you'll need some personal time off from work – say, if relatives are coming to town, or if you have an important religious holiday. Book the days off as far ahead as possible so your boss can schedule around it.

"Going down with stress"

Given the relatively low number of working hours and

the extensive social safety net, it might surprise you that the number of employees who "go down with stress" is extremely high in Denmark.

"Stress" is defined as being so overwhelmed with work or your working situation that you begin to suffer physical symptoms, such as insomnia or stomach pain. It's particularly common among female employees who are raising children in addition to working full-time, but it can happen to anyone, in particular people working in a poorly-defined job or with a difficult boss.

Many companies have stress hotlines you can call if you're starting to experience symptoms of stress. These are run by private health insurers engaged by the company and they claim to be 100% confidential. If you're feeling overwhelmed, call them earlier rather than later. The goal is to treat your stress before you fall apart entirely and have to take time off from work.

Your union may also offer counseling services, or will put you in touch with someone who can provide them.

When your colleague suffers from stress

Hotline or not, many workers do "go down with stress" and disappear from the office for weeks and sometimes months. When they come back, they often appear slightly fragile and will probably have shortened work hours.

Try not to be cynical about people suffering from stress or point out that hungry people in your home country know what stress really is. Stress is taken very seriously in Denmark.

Working with Denmark's neighbors: Norway, Sweden, Germany and more

When I first arrived in Denmark, it was common to attend a meeting in which Danes, Norwegians, and Swedes would each speak their own language and simply assume everyone else understood. It was a proud expression of Scandinavian solidarity.

Unfortunately it never worked very well, and everybody ended up understanding roughly 80% of what was being said. In particular, the Swedes and Norwegians struggled to puzzle out spoken Danish.

These days, the addition of other internationals to meetings means these inter-Scandinavian conversations are now conducted in English, to just about everyone's relief.

Norway: the poor kid is now rich

Many Danish companies co-operate extensively with their fellow Scandinavians in Sweden and Norway. The airline Scandinavian Air Services (SAS) flies with all three national flags on its planes, even though the Norwegian state sold its shares in the airline in 2018.

The Norwegian state is mighty and very rich. Norway was once the poor kid on the block, but after the discovery of North Sea oil, it became the neighborhood rich kid and in fact one of the richest countries in the world.

Many Danes go to Norway for work, in particular Danish healthcare workers, who can pocket hefty paychecks for a few weeks assisting patients in one of Norway's remote villages.

Norway was part of Denmark for three centuries and its

Royal Family is made up of leftover Danish Royals. In international sports competitions, Norway and Denmark are happy to cheer for each other once their own teams are eliminated.

They are less likely to cheer for Sweden, which is seen as the stiff, domineering big brother country that wants to tell everyone else what to do.

Sweden: Shocked at Danish directness

Sweden is indeed bigger, with a larger population and internationally-famous companies like IKEA and H&M. But many Swedes work in Denmark, particularly in Copenhagen, where they can commute to work over the Øresund Bridge.

In recent years, the Danish krone has been stronger than its Swedish counterpart, which means that a Danish salary can feel generous to someone who lives and pays their bills in Sweden.

Swedish and Danish working styles are different. Swedes tend to be much more formal than Danes – Swedish bosses certainly expect more deference than Danish ones do – and Swedes can be shocked at Danish directness.

The Swedish way is to dance around uncomfortable topics and blame any mistakes on a misguided consensus decision. Swedes spend much more time and effort trying to reach a consensus than Danes do, and once a consensus decision is reached, the team generally sticks to it.

Danes, on the other hand, will toss out a carefully-crafted group decision if conditions change or if they find something they think is better. This alarms Swedes.

Politeness and poise are valued in Sweden in a way they are not valued in Denmark, which is why Swedes often perceive Danes as irresponsible, unreliable, and sometimes rude.

They also sometimes see the Danes as racist and anti-foreigner, which is ironic because the flexibility of the Danish workplace means companies are more willing to take a chance on an unknown. If it doesn't work out, the employee can be quickly relieved of duty, but it is very difficult to fire someone in Sweden.

Finland and the Nordic region

Sometimes regional co-operation includes Finland and Iceland, which, in addition to the three Scandinavian countries, make up the Nordic region.

Finns are not Scandinavian and Finland's business cooperation with Denmark has had its ups and downs. The Finns are serious people, and the Danes are a bit more flexible (from the Danish point of view) or flaky (from the Finnish point of view.)

I was once part of a huge IT migration from a Finnish system to a Danish one that led to bad feelings on both sides. The Danes assumed they would sort out any problems as they went along, while the Finns expected a system that worked seamlessly from Day One.

Finns are sometimes less comfortable in English than their Nordic counterparts, and since they tend to be quiet people in the first place, misunderstandings can arise. One manager in Denmark told me that he'd let his team of Finnish workers discuss among themselves the solution to a problem, and then the team's best English speaker would communicate it.

Icelandic colleagues, plus Greenlanders and Faroese

It's also common to have colleagues from Iceland while working in Denmark. Many Icelandic children learn Danish at school – the country was under Danish rule for many years, only becoming fully independent in 1944 – and because Iceland is so small, Denmark is a clear choice for career opportunities.

You'll also meet Greenlanders and people from the Faroe Islands working in Denmark. Those two areas are Danish territories, so these people are Danish citizens, although they have their own languages and distinct cultures.

Other European colleagues: Trust vs protectiveness

In addition, you will meet ambitious young graduates from the Baltic countries (Estonia, Latvia, and Lithuania) and Poland building their career portfolios in Denmark, as well as many talents from Spain, Italy, Portugal, and Greece.

Some of these newcomers love the Danish working style of trust, flat hierarchy, and information sharing – and others struggle with it, having previously been more protective and competitive about their work.

In addition, people who come from countries with rampant corruption sometimes have trouble trusting Danish authorities, who are rarely corrupt, although they are sometimes very stubborn.

Germany: Tough history, cheerful present

Denmark's most important working relationship, however, is with its largest import and export partner: Germany.

Germany and Denmark have come to blows several times over the centuries, most recently during World War II, when Denmark was occupied by the Nazi army for five years. Older Danes put a candle in the window on the evening of May 4 to commemorate the occupation's end in 1945.

But there is surprisingly little rancor about this bloody history, and almost none expressed against contemporary Germans. Many Danish children choose to learn German in school, and Berlin and Munich are popular vacation destinations. Some trips are shorter: Danes love to drive across the border at Flensburg and get cut-rate beer and cigarettes in Germany.

A new underwater tunnel is being built between southern Denmark and northern Germany, which should bring the two countries even closer.

Structure and hierarchy

When it comes to working culture, Germans tend to be more structured than Danes. If there are ten steps to a working process, the Germans will want to carefully do each of them, while the Danes will merrily skip over the ones that don't offer an immediate payoff.

Danes have a relaxed nature which Germans appreciate in some contexts – they love to spend summers in Denmark, soaking up the sun on windy Danish beaches – but which also exasperates them when they want to get down to serious business.

One German entrepreneur I met in Denmark told me he had given up on hiring young Danes; according to him, they weren't always willing to show up for early-morning shifts, particularly on weekends. He blamed the Danish social welfare system for making them "too soft" and hired international students in Denmark instead.

Germans also tend to have more respect for hierarchy and titles than the Danes do. In Denmark, even medical doctors don't use "Dr." in front of their names, but only a fool would get between a German and their beloved "*Doktor*" title, whether the degree is in podiatry or poetry.

Managing Danes as an international

When I wrote the first edition of this book just five years ago, there was no need for a chapter about internationals managing Danes. There were relatively few international managers, and they were usually male CEOs hired from a neighboring country like Norway or the Netherlands.

That's changed quickly, and I now frequently meet managers who have been hired from throughout Europe as well as from Asia and the Americas. Many are women, and most have expertise in processes or technologies that make them a critical asset to Denmark.

Back in the day, some people believed that only Danes could manage Danes. Only Danes, they believed, could understand the quirkier aspects of Danish working culture.

Danish working culture is indeed quirky, but a gifted international manager can handle it, although internationals face some common challenges when they manage Danes.

Winning the team's trust

The first challenge is often winning over their Danish employees' trust. The international manager arrives confidently with a stellar CV, a record of accomplishment, and perhaps some weighty academic degrees as well, but the Danes aren't impressed.

They want to see what you can do.

One manager brought in with a far-reaching change mandate told me that she found her Danish team skeptical and somewhat grumpy until she completed and implemented one minor (and frankly insignificant) part of the project.

The team could now see with their own eyes that she was reliable and effective. They were much more cooperative going forward.

Nobody likes a star

Part of the problem is the sour anti-elitism that is the ugly side of Denmark's famous *Janteloven*. As a successful international manager, you were probably a top student during your school days, a top graduate at your respected university, and have since become a comet in your career field, delivering impressive results for the companies you've worked with. You're a star.

The problem is that in Denmark, people don't really like stars, or at least people who think they're stars or think they're better than anyone else. Being ambitious for one's product is fine, but a lust for personal power and prestige is considered unappealing. The commanding presence that works so well for you in many business cultures can be a turnoff for the egalitarian Danes.

And nobody will do anything just because you say so and you're the boss.

"Management by fear" doesn't work in Denmark

Motivating Danes is different than motivating workers in other countries. The social welfare state means there is no such thing as managing by fear: if an employee fails to carry out your directives and his services are terminated, he will still have full access to free health care, free university education for his children, and reasonable government income support for at least two years. You don't hold his financial security in the palm of your hand.

Individual recognition also isn't the motivator it is in some other cultures. There's no such thing as "employee of the month" in Denmark; Danes cringe at the idea of singling out one person for public praise or public criticism. They have worked in groups since the days of Viking ship crews, and much of the Danish educational system consists of group work. In the workplace, they succeed or fail as teams, not as individuals.

Danes like to give input

Instead, Danes are motivated by the ability to lend their expertise to a project. They expect to be consulted before you make just about any decision, and will be angry and annoyed if they are not asked about something they consider to be within their area of responsibility.

They will be happy to give you their input either in a formal group meeting or directly in a one-on-one conversation. In fact, they may jump over layers of management to volunteer the information or input they think you should have.

This unfortunately also works in the other direction: your superiors may jump over you to talk directly to your team when you're not around. Such is Danish egalitarianism and flat hierarchy.

Expect constant questions

The Danish educational system encourages students to constantly ask questions, and this habit continues into working life. Your team may openly question your approach and question your decisions. They would do the same for a Danish boss.

Danes hate micromanagement, so even though you as a manager will be telling them what to do, they will be very frosty if you tell them how to do it.

Fresh professional challenges are a motivator

It's important to come up with fresh professional challenges for your team, which Danes often value more than promotion up the hierarchy. While many cultures see a career path as a vertical climb to the top, Danes tend to see it as more horizontal and holistic, with new experiences and challenges outside the management path creating skills and depth.

Of course, some Danes would very much like to be promoted, but you may have to ask your Danish reports directly if they are interested in a higher position because they may not tell you themselves. Instead, you will be expected to simply notice how skilled they are. Danes like to believe that a good product sells itself.

If a position on your team comes up unexpectedly, pull them aside for a quick meeting and ask them if it is something they would like to be considered for. (Parents of small children sometimes say no.)

Time served versus productivity

The devotion to work-life balance in Denmark is something international managers will have to get used to. Team members really do leave the office at 4pm, or sometimes earlier; they will stay home for a few days if their child is ill; they will take every day of their vacations. I am often asked if Danes are lazy. They are not: they are hard workers. But they are not *hungry*.

A manager who equates hours on the job with productivity and effectiveness and who insists she wants to see more time in the office just for the sake of it will find herself very unpopular. The same is true for managers who schedule meetings outside the common working hours of roughly 9am to 3:30pm or ask the team to work on weekends or during vacation periods.

Finally, it's important to be compassionate to employees who need extra time off due to an emergency, such as a family member with a health crisis. The entire office will be watching how you treat this poor soul and assuming you would treat them the same way.

Colleagues are generally willing to help cover work tasks in the short term. If the employee needs more time off, consider hiring in temporary extra hands. Denmark has an army of freelancers and consultants who can be said goodbye to whenever you no longer need them.

Will I ever be promoted? Plus, how to leverage your annual review

I s the company you want to work for open to promoting you? Have other internationals who work for this company moved into management positions? These are questions worth asking at a job interview.

You're responsible for your own advancement

If the answer is "no," it doesn't mean you shouldn't take the job – just that you'll probably need to move to another company in order to advance. Many Danes do this too. It can be tough to suddenly become the boss of people who used to be your peers; it's often easier to start with an entirely new team.

It's important to keep in mind that you are responsible for your own advancement. In some countries with traditional corporate hierarchies, X number of years of experience may correlate with an almost guaranteed promotion, but this is not the case in Denmark.

The flat hierarchy in many Danish companies means there are simply fewer layers of management to move into. If you want a bigger role, you need to say so. A good time to do this is your annual employee review, required at most medium to large-size Danish companies.

Preparing for your annual review

At an annual review, each employee sits down with his or her boss to discuss their progress over the last year and plans for the next. They also deliver feedback on the boss's performance.

Preparing for the annual review often means filling out a

lot of forms before the review meeting, evaluating yourself as well as your boss.

I used to hate this part of the process when I worked at large corporations. Rating myself in an environment of *Janteloven* was always difficult – *Am I a 4 or a 5 out of 5 when it comes to quality of work? Can I allow myself to put 5?* – and the forms always seemed to be due at a time when I was busy with other stuff.

Had I been more ambitious to get into management, I would have been wasting an opportunity. The annual review is a great place to find out what plans the company has for you – if it has any plans for you at all.

Bring course requests to your annual review

Ask the company to pay for courses and training, whether it's a couple of day-long conferences or a full MBA. Look up the courses you want in advance and present them to your boss during the meeting, along with an explanation of how they will benefit your work.

Danes love continuing education, so if your company doesn't want to invest in training for you, it's a red flag that they don't see much of a future for you there. At one of my annual reviews, I asked for a specific course and was turned down ("too expensive"), only to find out that a colleague had been approved for the same course. I was out of that company within six months.

The good thing about courses is that the education you receive there – and the contacts you make – are easily transferable to your next job. A recent course makes you look "fresh" to a potential employer, particularly if it's the first educational certificate you've picked up in Denmark as opposed to yourhome country.

The salary review meeting

Many companies have now removed any discussion of salary from the annual review and created a separate salary review meeting.

Prepare for this meeting thoroughly, with statistics from your union showing how much people with your skills and experience are earning.

And be ready to show how you've gone beyond the basic requirements of the job by creating new products or processes, saving the company money, or bringing in new customers.

In Denmark, you generally don't get a raise just for time served, unless one has been negotiated by your union for all its members. You'll need to convince your boss – and she'll need to convince her boss – that you're worth the extra dough.

Consider working for yourself

If you don't see a path to promotion at your current company but aren't ready to leave yet, consider starting your own side business, or "B-job," as the Danes call it.

Check, of course, to make sure your visa allows for this and that the HR department at your corporate "A-job" approves. You will probably have to choose a B-job that has nothing to do with your main job and can be completed outside working hours.

Working for yourself is common in Denmark; tens of thousands of Danes do it. You can set up a one-person company online in less than 24 hours, and the tax ramifications are not as complicated as they are in many other countries. You'll also be able to write off business-related purchases like computers and smartphones against your company profits.

Should you end up leaving your corporate job for any reason, your B-job may suddenly become your main source of income.

Can I date my Danish colleague?

Many Danes meet their future spouses at work. Yet there are also strict laws in Denmark against sexual harassment.

Where do you draw a line between harassment and two adults developing tender feelings for each other?

Keep your hands to yourself in the office

First of all, the obvious: you are not allowed to touch your colleagues where they don't want to be touched. (A good general rule is to stay away from everything except hands and shoulders).

And you are certainly not allowed to imply that the people who work for you can enhance their careers by spending one-on-one time with you outside of the office.

Furthermore, it's important to remember that the laws of romance common in many cultures do not apply to Denmark.

Poems, flowers, and other gifts of the heart are uncommon and can be seen as a little aggressive. And Danish men and women do not play "hard to get." If you get a sense that someone is going out of their way to avoid you at team lunches or other social events, it's not because they want to intrigue you. It's because you're making them uncomfortable.

Unlike in some cultures, a "no" in Denmark really is a no. It's not an invitation to keep trying.

A good way to get to know someone

With that in mind, meeting someone at work can be the start of a long and happy relationship.

You'll get to know them in a relaxed group environment and see how they handle a variety of different situations and challenges.

Keep in mind that in Denmark it is often the woman who takes the initiative.

It sometimes starts with alcohol

Given the Danes' fondness for alcohol, many interoffice romances start at the annual Christmas party. Ms. X and Mr. Y drink a bottle of wine or two, wiggle suggestively together on the dance floor, and depart to one or the other's home in a taxi to complete the evening. The next morning, they discuss whether they are interested in a future romantic relationship.

If that doesn't sound like your style, or if Christmas is too far away, there are other ways to handle the matter.

How to ask your colleague on a date

For example, if you have your eye on Mr. Y., you can use your team lunches together to find out if he's single and, if so, what he likes to do on weekends. If he likes professional handball, classical art, or monster movies, find an event that's happening two or three weeks from now and ask if he'd like to attend it with you.

(Never ask a Dane to attend something with you last-minute: they are not spontaneous people and often have their calendars arranged weeks in advance.)

Even if Mr. Y says no, he now knows you're interested in meeting outside office hours, in what the Danes call "private time," aka personal time. He can then ask you for a get-together outside the office if he's so inclined.

Alternately, you can wait a month or two and then invite

him to another event. If he says no again, he's not interested, and you should leave him alone. Further date requests could be seen as harassment.

Should you tell your colleagues about your romance?

Most couples who meet in the office in Denmark keep their romance to themselves for the first few months. Some don't announce it until they have a major life event, such as moving in together, a wedding, or a baby on the way.

Danes have a great respect for privacy and dislike gossip, so even if your colleagues suspect that there may be something going on between you, they are unlikely to bring it up. As long as you don't blow kisses to each other in the office or have screaming fights about who overcooked the previous night's dinner, they will do their best to stay out of it. Even colleagues that accidentally spot you two in local restaurants or movie theaters will usually keep it to themselves.

The one exception is a boss dating a person he or she directly supervises. The boss half of this relationship should report it to their supervisor, or HR, after a month or so of loving togetherness, especially if the relationship looks like it could become long-term.

If that happens, and if the company is big enough, one half of the couple usually transfers to another department or team.

Trailing spouses and working in Denmark

If you're coming from abroad to work in Denmark, you may be bringing along your spouse. That can be great – it's nice to have someone to shiver through the Danish summer with.

But an unhappy spouse is one of the main reasons why people who come to work in Denmark end up leaving.

Denmark is not an easy place to make friends, given that Danish culture tends toward "respecting your privacy" by not striking up conversations with strangers.

It can also be tough for spouses to get jobs in Denmark, particularly well-educated spouses seeking jobs at their level of expertise.

Single-earner households are rare

A generation ago, expat spouses were mostly stay-at-home-wives who supported their husbands' careers.

Spouses are different today. Most come to Denmark after finishing their advanced education, and they are sometimes mid-career. A good portion of them are men.

Most contemporary spouses don't want to stay at home and, even if they did, that's rarely affordable in Denmark. The Danish tax structure makes single-earner households a rarity. Even if the person working has a generous salary, a big chunk of that income will go to taxes. Prices are high in Denmark for rent, food, and other daily necessities.

Besides, stay-at-home spouses don't really have a role in Danish society, as they do in many other cultures. There's no need to stay home and care for small children: Danish kids start full-time daycare when they are about a year old. (Not sending your child to daycare is considered very poor parenting in Denmark, since daycare is where the kids learn Danish and learn the social rules that are so important to Danish culture. Even the children of the Danish Royal Family go to daycare.)

And because there are so few other stay-at-home spouses, people who choose to stay at home can find themselves very lonely.

The working spouse has colleagues and business connections to help them ease into Danish culture. The non-working spouse can feel adrift.

Volunteering – if you can afford it

If your family's financial situation permits it, consider having the trailing spouse commit to an ongoing volunteer role.

Spejders, the Danish equivalent of Scouts or Guides, are always looking for adults to help children explore the outdoors.

And the independent sports clubs that make up the steel skeleton of Danish social life – football, volleyball, judo – need people to serve as trainers, or take on organizational work.

Spouses can also get involved in short-term volunteering for events like the Copenhagen Film Festival or Vejle by Night, where they'll have a chance to make new contacts.

Finding a job for a trailing spouse

Finding a job for a trailing spouse isn't easy in Denmark, even if that spouse is highly educated, and especially if the spouse's partner is on a limited-term contract.

Even though the average Danish employee usually switches jobs every two to three years, employers can be frightened by the knowledge that you're actively planning to leave in two or three years.

A good tip is to look for *barselsvikariat*. These are short-term jobs to cover for employees on parental leave, so they're naturally limited in time.

Another option is to lie – or to slightly slant the truth. Instead of, "My spouse has a two-year contract" you can say, "Well, we're starting with two years. But we love Denmark for so many reasons..." and go on to list some of those reasons. You'll never go wrong as a foreigner by telling a Dane how much you love Denmark.

Some spouses find jobs at large companies that have English as a corporate language, or with non-governmental organizations based in Copenhagen. But that's not practical for everyone, particularly if your spouse's job keeps you in Jutland.

You could try leveraging your native language – working, for example, as a Finnish-speaking customer service rep to help the Finnish customers of a Danish firm.

Job-hunting at smaller companies

The harsh fact is that spouses will probably have to lower their expectations when looking for a job. That sounds counterintuitive in a country with many high-tech industries screaming about the need for highly-educated workers, but it's the direct experience of many people working with spouse placement.

You'll probably have to look for jobs at smaller companies, where the employees might all be Danish and might not be entirely comfortable speaking English.

That discomfort means that you may need to start with a six-month unpaid placement that will allow the company to discover how many wonderful things you can contribute.

Local *bosætningskonsulenter* – settlement consultants – can help you find this kind of placement.

The elevator speech

Spouses who are looking for a job in Denmark – really, anyone who is looking for a job in Denmark – should also have a 15-20 word "elevator speech" about what they can do.

Focus on what you can offer a business, not on your degrees. "I want to help small companies work with online procurement, and I'm very interested in sustainability" is much better than "I have an MSc in Computer Science."

This short speech can be used during social occasions and other unofficial networking opportunities – and most hiring in Denmark is done by networking. Your partner's colleague, your child's daycare provider, or the guy pouring your coffee may know someone looking for someone like you.

Spouses should also have a well-written LinkedIn profile ready to impress anyone who might have a job for them.

Distance working as an option

A spouse can also avoid the Danish labor market entirely by doing distance work. Illustration, freelance writing, and programming can basically be done from anywhere, although as a resident of Denmark, you'll still be responsible for paying Danish taxes on your income. (That can be a handicap if you compete on price, because the people you're competing with usually do not pay giant Danish taxes and are often willing to work for less.)

Alternately, your time in Denmark can be a good chance to finally complete that Masters' degree or Ph.D., particularly since tuition is usually tax-financed and free for the student. Your fellow students will also provide you with a social network, which will make your time in Denmark happier.

If all else fails, write a book.

Staying happy is key

Whatever your approach, keeping yourself happy and engaged in Danish society will be a major factor in your spouse's success in Denmark.

To avoid becoming too isolated, you might need to re-establish old hobbies. If you used to love squash or played upright bass in a jazz band, now might be the time to take it up again. Helping plan neighborhood events is a good way to make friends. So are your free introductory Danish language classes or Facebook groups for spouses in your area.

Introverted spouses will probably have the hardest time. Danes see friendship as a lifelong relationship, so they're unlikely to invest emotions in someone they fear will only be around for a couple of years or so. They may seem cold, but the truth is they just don't want to start something they're not sure they can finish.

Most of your initial social contacts will probably be expats or sometimes Danes who have lived in your country. At the very least, these types of people will be able to sympathize when you complain about the dreadful Danish weather.

The Danish art of taking time off

Taking time off is a very important part of Danish life – in fact, some people would say it is one of the best parts of Danish life.

The best example, of course, is the famous Danish summer vacation. Around April or May, people begin asking, "Are you taking three or four?"

What they mean is, *Are you taking three or four weeks off for your summer vacation?*

Vacation as a human right

In the United States, where I come from, even taking two weeks off is extravagant. You always have the feeling that if you're gone too long, there may not be a job waiting for you when you get back.

In Denmark, a long summer vacation is baked into the business calendar. If you have a full-time job, you get five weeks annual vacation, and your boss is legally required to allow you to take three of those weeks sometime between May 1 and September 30.

Many Danes consider a vacation to be a human right. Even if you're unemployed, you get paid time off from looking for a job so you can enjoy a vacation in the summer. If you get sick during your vacation, you can even request more time off to compensate.

That's the social welfare state – I hope you enjoy paying taxes to support it.

Time off makes for great small talk

Ironically, the people who pay the most taxes don't always get to enjoy the longest vacations. People who work for themselves, like me, take relatively little vacation – I took ten days this summer, and I know other busy self-employed people who took none at all.

But vacation is still a very important part of Danish culture. You can always make small talk with a Dane you don't know very well by asking where she went on her last vacation or where she intends to go on her next one.

There's fall vacation in October, aligned with the fall school break, and of course, Christmas vacation, which usually lasts two weeks. Winter vacation is in February (maybe a ski trip), and there are a minimum of five days off over Easter, plus some odd one-day holidays speckled through May.

This doesn't mean everybody travels every time. You might do a renovation project around the house – Danes have a passion for fixing up their houses – or spend time in the summer house, or attend some big family event like a wedding, a confirmation, or an 80th birthday party.

Vacations are often expressed in week numbers, with Week 1 beginning in January and Week 52 rounding up December. Your colleague may tell you, for example, that she will be taking "Week 42" off to install her new kitchen. Changing the settings on your phone or laptop calendar to show week numbers makes this system easier to follow.

Strategic timing of your vacations

If you work on a team with several people, you'll have to agree who gets to take which weeks off on vacation. Reserve as far in advance as possible; your colleagues will.

And choosing your optimum vacation time requires a little knowledge of Danish culture.

For example, the last two weeks in July are a dead zone for business in Denmark; many companies close down entirely. If you're able to stay on the job during this period, it's a great time to get some peace and quiet around the office. Commuting is easy – the streets of many big cities are empty – and you can finalize big projects without being interrupted by meetings. Or you can just tidy your desk and organize the files on your computer.

I used to do this a lot before my daughter started school and my vacation opportunities were suddenly limited to the school summer holidays. School summer holidays usually last about six weeks, from late June to early August, and prices for airfare out of Denmark and places to stay within Denmark double during this period.

If you don't have kids, or if your children are too young for school, you can save a lot of money by scheduling your "summer" vacation in May or September. Your colleagues with school-age children will thank you.

The risk of working during other people's vacation

Other times the office will be dead include the three days before Easter and the week between Christmas and New Year's. If you're not doing anything else, this is usually a convenient way to get full pay for some slow days at the office.

Occasionally, though, some unexpected situation can come crashing down on your head, and you will be the only one around to handle it. If it does, it is considered poor style to call your boss and interrupt her vacation. Unless it's an emergency, time off in Denmark is sacred.

Leave work on time

Even outside of your vacations, you can start enjoying the Danish way of taking time off. You can leave work precisely at 4pm – or at 3:30pm on Fridays. You can avoid working evenings or weekends. And you can mostly ignore business calls after hours and neglect to answer business emails when you're not in the office – except maybe on a Sunday night, the unofficial follow-up deadline for mails sent the previous week.

With some exceptions, the Danish way to spend time off is with your family. And if you don't have a family, with your hiking club, or with friends from your salsa-dancing class, or out in the garden painting watercolors.

Otherwise, you can always fix up your house.

Epilogue: The bad news about working in Denmark (Why many internationals leave)

I f you're frustrated about your working situation in Denmark, take an afternoon off to visit one of the country's dustier museums. (I did a lot of this in the year I was unemployed in Denmark.)

The Workers' Museum in Copenhagen is a good choice, but so is the *Gamle By* (Old Town Museum) in Aarhus or the Esbjerg City Museum. Don't go to see anything fancy like ARoS in Aarhus or Brandts in Odense – these are museums that show Denmark as hip, cool, and wealthy.

Instead, choose a museum that gives you a sense of how poor and desperate Denmark used to be.

One of the poorest countries in Europe

Denmark was once among the poorest countries in Europe. Most of the country was dependent on agriculture in a harsh climate with a short growing season, or on fishing from dangerous seas.

Learning to work together as a tight-knit group of fishermen or farmers often made the difference between starvation and survival.

It's this same group instinct that can make foreigners feel like outsiders today.

The difficulty of being an outsider

When you're dependent on the group for food, shelter, and safety, as Danes were for generations, you need to be able to trust the other members of the group.

An outsider, by definition, needs to earn that trust.

The Danes don't always make it easy. The "yin" of *Janteloven*, the well-enforced law of personal humility, is matched by the "yang" of deep national certainty that the Danish way of doing things is generally best.

This can be true on an office level or on a societal level. *It's always worked this way for us before! Why should you, an outsider, propose anything different?*

The reason, of course, is that an outsider has arrived from a world of eight billion people, many of whom have great ideas that a country of 5.8 million might not be familiar with.

But convincing a Danish employer of this, particularly a Danish employer that is successful in its field, can be difficult to impossible.

A sense of defenselessness

Denmark may be a destination country for now, but it wasn't long ago that its own citizens were so poor and hungry that they were forced to leave home.

On your trip to the dusty museum, you will see some of the poverty that prompted hundreds of thousands of Danes (about 15% of the population at the time) to flee the country in the late 1800s, mostly to the US and Canada.

Much of this emigration was set off by a humiliating military loss to Germany in 1864, which was the last time the Danish military tried to defend its territory.

This sense of helplessness is still part of the Danish DNA, as is the country's occupation by Germany during World War II.

Danes feel, in many ways, that their small country is defenseless from the outside world. Instead, they set up small and medium-sized barriers to try to defend what seems to them to be a good and worthwhile way of life, as evidenced by a generous social welfare state.

Some of these barriers may feel like they're designed to keep you out, on a legal basis, a personal basis, or both.

Leaving Denmark

If you've chosen to leave Denmark, you're not alone. Many foreigners leave because their job contracts have run out, their relationship with a Dane has ended, or because they just don't believe they'll ever feel at home here.

The Danish government has helpfully prepared a page full of practical steps you need to take when leaving Denmark, such as de-registering your CPR number and notifying your child's school and the tax authorities. It's a good idea to tell your Danish business contacts you are leaving but keep the relationship intact; you never know when you might be asked to take on a Danish project from your home country.

But it is just as important to manage your own feelings about leaving Denmark.

Online forums feature plenty of expats who are still stewing about their bad experiences, people who are bitter about everything from the supposed unfriendliness of the Danes to the lack of public-service websites in English to the overabundance of calcium in the tap water.

Depart with good memories

The best thing you can do for yourself when leaving Denmark is to depart with good memories. Even if something went wrong, or several things went wrong, you have the power to focus on the good things and the good times.

Something must have been good, right? The wonderful fresh Danish pastries? The green city parks on one of the few days of warm sunshine? The windy Danish beaches with their pale, clean sand?

Maybe it was the colorful lights and excitement of Tivoli at Christmastime, or the ease of riding your bike through the city in a safe, well-paved bike lane. Maybe it was the sleek, practical design of the Danish housewares and home fixtures. Maybe it was the friendliness shown to your children in even the fanciest restaurants.

If you decide to leave Denmark, the best thing you can do for yourself is focus on the good memories and expend less energy on the bad ones.

And think about how lucky you are to never again have to shiver through a chilly, gray Danish November.

Or a chilly, gray Danish July.

About the Author

Kay Xander Mellish is a speaker, writer, and cultural coach based in Copenhagen, Denmark. Her "How to Live in Denmark" podcast has run for more than ten years, with more than two million downloads.

A native of Wauwatosa, Wisconsin, USA, Kay studied journalism and art history at New York University.

She worked for several US Fortune 500 companies, including units of Disney and News Corp., before moving to Denmark where she held jobs at Carlsberg and Danske Bank.

Since 2012, she has worked as a consultant to a variety of small, medium, and large-size Danish companies on communications and culture assignments and coached both newcomers to Denmark and Danes moving overseas.

Kay now offers presentations and workshops on Danish culture, in particular Danish working culture, to companies and organizations.

She is available for both in-person and virtual events through her website, www.kxmgroup.dk.

ALSO BY KAY XANDER MELLISH

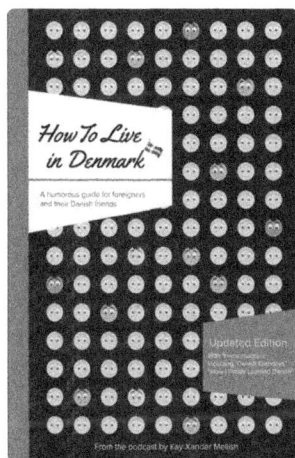

How to Live in Denmark

In this popular book based on the "How to Live in Denmark" podcast, Kay draws on her own experiences as a foreigner in Denmark when it comes to learning Danish, making friends in Denmark, and looking for a place to live in Copenhagen. She also touches on dating in Denmark, Danish drinking culture, Danish child-raising, and how you can guess a Danish person's age from their first name alone.

ALSO BY KAY XANDER MELLISH

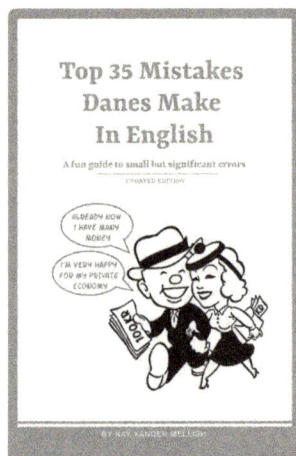

Top 35 Mistakes Danes Make in English

Danes speak wonderful English, yet they make a few common mistakes over and over. Whether it's telling the DJ to "screw up the music," mixing up "customer" and "costumer," or using the expression 'I've tried' for unplanned experiences ("I've also tried breaking my leg"), these mistakes are easy to fix, making Danes' spoken and written English even smoother and more impressive. This short, light-hearted book will help.

ALSO BY KAY XANDER MELLISH

Working with Danes: Tips for Americans

Denmark is a great place to do business. Infrastructure is good, corruption is minimal, innovation is respected, and business structures are flexible. Most people speak excellent English. Still, many Americans get off on the wrong foot – sometimes just by being too upbeat, too enthusiastic, too *American*.

Working with Americans: Tips for Danes

Doing business in the US is challenging and exciting. The size, wealth, and diversity of the American market is hard to beat. But when it comes to business culture, too many Danes assume that the US is basically just like Denmark – only bigger. This can be the first of many expensive mistakes.

Acknowledgements

Thanks to Kate Dahl, Anatolie Cantir, Anne Katrine Skovenborg, Annette Dahl, Burkhart Franz, Louise Nielsen, Signe Ørom, and Dennis Nørmark for the many insights they have shared with me about Danish culture and Danish working culture over the years.

Many thanks also to my beta readers, Lea Lønsted, Nancy Zhang, Susie Hjorth, Stjepan Mikulić, Karl Peter Vilandt, and Louise Courtnadge for their useful suggestions and insights.